MW00678790

Cornbread & Caviar
A Final Taste

Sermons and Remembrances of Bob Jones Jr.

Bob Jones University Press
Greenville, South Carolina 29614

Cornbread and Caviar . . . A Final Taste
Sermons and Remembrances of Bob Jones Jr.

Designer: Chris Hartzler
Project Editor: Mark Sidwell

© 1998 Bob Jones University Press
Greenville, South Carolina 29614

Printed in the United States of America
All rights reserved

ISBN 1-57924-082-8

15   14   13   12   11   10   9   8   7   6   5   4   3   2   1

Without the editorial assistance of Mrs. Mildred Butts, this book would have been impossible. She compiled and edited the anecdotes and sermons.

For ten years she was my grandfather's secretary and in more recent years has given valued office assistance to both my father and me. She and her husband, Tom, have served the Lord faithfully at BJU for a combined total of eighty-five years. Their lives and influence have profoundly affected several generations of Christian college students. Their imprint on BJU is indelible. Without them and others like them, BJU would not be what it is today.

—Bob Jones III

Perhaps Dad's most enduring legacy for the generations to come, if Christ tarries, will be his poetry and hymns. Below is a facsimile of his last written words, an unfinished poem, which I have presumed to complete (opposite page—the italicized words are mine) and for which Dr. Dwight Gustafson, who was dean of the School of Fine Arts at Bob Jones University for forty-three years and musical collaborator with Dad on many of his poems, has done a hymn setting (the page following).

—*Bob Jones III*

WYNDHAM GARDEN HOTELS

O, The privilege of the prophets
Upon Whom the Spirit Came
In the voice of Inspiration
Speaking Wonders in God's ...

O, The Courage of the Martyrs,
Who by death confirmed their witness

O the Wealth of the Apostles
In their Master's presence found
As His simple ~~sharing~~ Sharing
~~all~~ Joys of Heaven ~~crowd around.~~
                    fell around.

Parting Wonder

O the *power* of the prophets
Upon whom the Spirit came
In the voice of inspiration,
Speaking wonders in God's name.

O the courage of the martyrs
Given grace from God above,
In the fiery furnace tested,
Standing strong in heaven's love.

O the wealth of the apostles
In their Master's presence found,
As His simple service sharing
Joys of heaven all around.

O the future of the ransomed
Safely found on heaven's shore,
Purchased heirs of Calvary's pardon,
Heaven's Christ they now adore.

O dear Master, kindly use me
Someway showing praise to Thee.
O dear Savior, ever find me
Leading sinners unto Thee.

O the Power of the Prophets

PARTING WONDER

Bob Jones Jr. *(1911-97)*
Bob Jones III *(b. 1939)*

Dwight Gustafson
(b. 1930)

O the pow-er of the proph-ets Up-on whom the Spir-it
O the cour-age of the mar-tyrs Giv-en grace from God a-
O the wealth of the a-pos-tles In their Mas-ter's pres-ence
O the fu-ture of the ran-somed Safe-ly found on heav-en's

came In the voice of in-spir-a-tion, Speak-ing won-ders in God's
bove, In the fier-y fur-nace test-ed, Stand-ing strong in heav-en's
found, As His sim-ple serv-ice shar-ing Joys of hea-ven all a-
shore, Pur-chased heirs of Cal-va-ry's par-don, Hea-ven's Christ they now a-

name.
love.
round.   O dear Mas-ter, kind-ly use me, Some-way show-ing praise to
dore.

Thee. O dear Sav-ior, ev-er find me Lead-ing sin-ners un-to Thee.

© 1998 by Bob Jones University.
All Rights Reserved.

Contents

Preface

His autobiography, *Cornbread and Caviar,* was Dad's honest, unembellished story of a life that was as humanly weak and sinfully flawed as any of ours. But it was also a cross-ransomed life with surrendered talents and selfless service under the control of the Holy Spirit for the glory of God and the proclamation of His Son, our Savior, Jesus Christ.

There were two sides to my father's life. The caviar of his rare and delectable style of preaching filled with metaphor made the passages of Scripture leap from the page and impress themselves on the heart and mind of the hearer, often seemingly taking him to the very presence of God. As they exulted in the glories of Christ, his sermons made us breathe celestial air and feel the streets of gold beneath our feet. As far as I know, no other preacher with a style like his is on the scene today. A few favorite samples of that caviar are included in this book for the tasting.

But it was the cornbread side of Dad that made him so lovable. It was his very human side, which could easily tease, sometimes shock, and frequently surprise with unwarranted kindness and gifts. It was the part of him that was companion to the twinkle in his eyes, the outspokenness of his convictions, and the overflowing love of his heart. It was the part that couldn't pass a delicatessen or a candy store without buying an infinite variety of kosher dill pickles, cheeses, jelly beans, chocolates, or any of the other many things he was so greatly fond of—always more than he could eat in a week and, therefore, copiously shared with everybody in sight. A lot of the cornbread will be found in this book in the form of anecdotes submitted by graduates and friends from around the world who knew him in varied personal and ministry settings.

I liked the cornbread part of him that overflowed with surprises, such as a birthday or Christmas present given months ahead of time because he had bought it in some faraway place and was so excited to see the look on the recipient's face that he just couldn't bring himself to hang onto it until the event arrived for which it was purchased. He would give it with a promise that it was an "early" present, but then either his forgetfulness or his generosity caused him to come up with something else when the occasion finally arrived. In his bag of surprises was a piece of fun he liked to spring on unsuspecting members of the numerous tour groups Dad led to the Holy Land or elsewhere. On occasion, he would offer someone a luscious-looking chocolate-covered cherry containing a small dab of liqueur and revel with laughter over the look on the face of the innocent recipient as he grimaced and shed tears from the burning in his throat. Dad's unpredictability made him fascinating. Boring he was not!

He was part of Bob Jones University for the first seventy-one years of its ministry, and his cultural and artistic imprints are seen everywhere on this campus but are nowhere more apparent than in the world-acclaimed collection of almost 450 paintings of sacred art by the old masters. His life without pretense; his tender approachableness; his generosity and concern for everyone who loved the Lord, especially the students and faculty; and his unflinching, two-fisted, "tell it as you see it" approach to life and ministry all blended to make him "just folks"—just cornbread.

When those of you who knew him visit his grave on the fountain island at the center of campus, I hope you will feel, as Mother and all the family do, that the twelve words inscribed on his marker appropriately describe this man of God as you knew him.

> A prophet's eye
> A poet's voice
> A servant's hands
> A ransomed soul

Sermons

Bow at a Venture
II Chronicles 18:33

"And a certain man drew a bow at a venture, and smote the king of Israel between the joints of the harness." That's all; just that sentence. Here is a situation where two men had gathered together to make themselves allies in a war. One of them is the king of Israel, Ahab—evil, ungodly man; Ahab, the apostate; Ahab, the man who brought evil upon his country and upon his family; a man who married the wrong wife and let her run him and run the kingdom. The other man is the king of Judah, God's man whom God has blessed and prospered and who had no business whatsoever in making this alliance with this ungodly king, for God forbids the godly to be aligned with the ungodly and God's people to line up with the enemies of the Almighty. They are having a big occasion before they go forth to battle. The thrones of the kings are set up in kind of a square before the gate of the city, and they have all of the prophets, Ahab's prophets, to come along to tell them whether or not they are going to be successful in the battle; and that is a great ecumenical occasion. They are all in complete agreement. They all say, "Oh, yes, go up; you will win this battle." And one man takes a pair of horns and puts them on his forehead and dances around and says, "This is the way you are going to push back the enemy." Oh, it is a great occasion.

But the king of Judah is not impressed. He senses that this thing is not of God, and he says to Ahab, "Have you no prophet of God in this land?"

"Yes," he says, "we have got one, but he's no good. He never prophesies anything good to me." Thank God for that! God's man cannot prophesy good to the ungodly. There is nothing worse than a servant of God who promises God's blessing on the ungodly, because God's man is supposed to speak God's Word and represent God's Truth. "Well," he says, "send for this man."

They send for him, and he comes; and on the way there, the man who brings him says in effect, "Look, won't you try to be nice just one time? Don't say something unpleasant. Don't break the spirit of this occasion. Agree with the prophets of Baal. It will be a great thing. Tell the kings to go up to battle and they will win it." Well, they come, and the man speaks. "Yes," he says, "go on up." In other words, "You have made up your mind; go on up."

The king of Judah looks at him and says, "I command you to tell me the truth. What does God have to say about this?" And the prophet of God says, "God has to say that if you go up in this battle, Ahab is going to die as a result of this battle. It is going to be a terrible defeat." Ahab, of course, was furious; and he said, "You put this man in jail on bread and water, and when I get back, I'll take care of him." But he never came back because no man comes back when God pronounces judgment upon him. Young people, one thing is as certain as that the sun will rise tomorrow if the world holds together, and that is that God's program no man can defeat. You can make up your mind to it. You can ride in the chariot of victory with God, or you can be crushed by the wheels of that chariot; but God's program is going to move on. Everything that God declares shall be performed. His word is "yea and amen," and the Word is ever fixed in heaven. Not a jot or a tittle will pass away until all shall be fulfilled.

You remember the story of Joseph? He was a foolish boy; he bragged too much. He thought his brothers would be interested in his dreams. They weren't interested in his dreams because his dreams all lifted him up and put them down. He said, "Let me tell you what I dreamed. I dreamed that all the sheaves of the field, your sheaves and Dad's and Mother's, all bowed down to my sheaf." He had dreams like that, and he told them. The brothers came to hate him. He was the father's favorite.

One day the brothers were away looking after the sheep, far from home. The father sent Joseph up there to see how they were getting on. They saw him coming a long way off and said, "Here comes this dreamer." Listen, it is a wonderful thing to be a dreamer. I am not talking about daydreams now, but I am talking about the dreams that flood a man's soul, that lift him. Everything that was ever accomplished began with a dream in somebody's heart. Don't ever be ashamed of the man who has high dreams and high hopes if they are godly dreams and godly hopes. These brothers said, "We will get rid of this fellow." They decided they would kill him, and then one of them said, "No, let's don't kill him. Let's put him down in this dry well here." So they put him down in the dry well. By and by one of the brothers hoped to come back to free him when the other brothers had gone to sleep (one good brother in the crowd). He left him there. A group of slave traders came along on their way to Egypt, and some of the brothers said, "Hey, look. Why don't we sell this guy down to Egypt?" "All right, let's do that. We'll make some money off him. We will take his coat and dip it in blood and take it home to Dad and tell him that we found it on the road—that a wild beast got Joseph." So they sold him, and he was taken down to Egypt. The father's heart was broken when he saw the bloody cloak.

But God put Joseph in Egypt. Those boys simply bought him a ticket to get him there. He got to Egypt and became the doer of everything in the house of the man to whom he was sold. But the man's wife lied about him, and he went to jail. We are told that in the jail everything that was done, Joseph was the doer. One day he stood before Pharaoh. Pharaoh had had a dream, and Joseph interpreted Pharaoh's dream. He said, "There are going to be seven rich years in this land with much crops; then there are going to be seven years of famine." "What will I do about it?" "Well, you had better have great granaries built and save the crops from this seven years because you are going to need them in the second seven years." And Pharaoh made Joseph (this young man who had been brought down there by slave traders) the second in command in Egypt. Joseph saved all of the Middle East in the terrible years of famine and was able to return good for evil to his brothers. He brought his father and all his brethren down to Egypt and was reunited with them. Don't you feel anybody can do harm to you if you are in the will of God. No matter what they try to do to you, if you are in the place of God's appointment, God is going to see that His purpose in your life is fulfilled. You remember that when the going gets tough and the times are hard and you are in the midst of difficulties and can't find a way out. Just trust the Lord. He will take care of you.

Four hundred years went by in Egypt. There was now a pharaoh who no longer remembered Joseph, and Joseph's people are in slavery. They are working to make bricks, working in the mud pits and the slime pits. Still they prosper and grow. Pharaoh said, "I've got to do something about this. These slave people are going to take over my kingdom. I'm going to have all the boy babies killed at birth." And he gave the order. But there was one Jewish mother who set her mother's heart against the king's command and said, "He's not going to get my little Moses." She hid him.

When he got a little bigger, she said, "Now, I'm going to fix him where nobody will find him." So she made a basket and put pitch on the outside and lined it with some soft linen. She put the baby in it and hid it down in the bulrushes on the edge of the Nile. She put his sister to watch over little Moses, who was hidden by the high reeds. Pharaoh's daughter had a favorite bathing place at the Nile where the marble stairs of the great palace went down to the river; but on this day, she was out walking and decided to go swimming in another place, and she was looking along the bank of the Nile when she heard a baby cry. "Go get that." They brought the little baby to her. You know the story. The result is that Moses was introduced into Pharaoh's house, the eventual heir to the throne, and put in the place of power where he had access as a prince of Egypt when he came back to stand before Pharaoh.

God handled that matter. God kept the currents of the Nile so still that the little baby's boat did not float away. He protected it from the crocodiles in the river's marsh, and He sent Pharaoh's daughter there at the right time, and God breathed a little cry into the baby's mouth. Listen, God handles all nature and the devices of kings and queens and princes in order to perform His purpose.

You remember the story of Balak. Balak said, "I am going to have to do something to get rid of all these people. They are coming across my land now." The Israelites had been set free, and Moses had led them out of the land of Egypt, almost to the Promised Land. They were on the verge of reaching that, and Balak said, "If these people who are swelling out over my kingdom by the hundreds of thousands aren't moved, something is going to happen. There won't be any food left for my people." So he sent for Balaam to curse them, and Balaam came and stood before the king—this king Balak, who had said, "Peradventure I shall prevail." Say, that is a lovely word, "peradventure." It is the gambler's word—there is a chance; it may be; perhaps. It is a good word. "Peradventure, by chance, this may come to be." But, my friend, there is no "chance" in the program of God. God's program is inflexible, and God moves along the path of His purpose. Balak wanted to curse the people, but he couldn't curse them. How could he curse them when God was blessing them? Every time Balaam opened his mouth to curse these people for Balak, blessing came out, and more blessing poured out, and more blessing . . . peradventure.

Remember the story of Jonah? God said, "Jonah, you go and preach to Nineveh, that great city." But Jonah didn't want to go. He's the only evangelist I ever heard of who didn't want to take a citywide campaign in the biggest city of the world. He said to himself, "I know what is going to happen. I will go there and preach, and those people will repent; and God will spare them, and I'll look like a fool." What could make a preacher happier than to see people repent and come out from under the judgment of God? So Jonah went down and found a ship to Tarshish. That's the way it is put—he "found" a ship. There were lots of ships in the harbor. There is a boat that has just come down from Tyre and Sidon, a boat with purple sails. It is not ready to go anywhere. There is another ship there pulled up on the beach, and they are caulking the seams. It's not ready to go. There is only one ship in the harbor that is ready to go, and it will be going just to the place that Jonah wants to go—way out to the coast of Spain, as far as man could go in that inland sea, way out to the Straits of Gibraltar to the Gates of Hercules. Jonah said, "Well, I'm lucky. I am going to get away from God." And he paid his fare and went aboard. Then he went down inside and went to sleep.

How could he sleep—this man whom God had sent on a mission of mercy and of grace and of judgment? Now he's trying to get away from God. They pull up the anchor, cast off the hawsers, raise the sails, and set out. But they are not on their way to Spain. They thought they were, but God had other arrangements. They got out to sea and a storm came up. The sails were torn and the masts were broken, and they started throwing cargo overboard in order to lighten the ship. Then they cast lots to see who had caused this storm to come, and the lot fell on Jonah. He said, "Yeah, throw me overboard. God sent this storm because of me." At least he had enough grace to admit he was to blame. Those pagan sailors hated to throw him overboard, but they finally did. But God had a submarine already chartered, a great fish. It opened its mouth and took Jonah in. I believe, as I read the passage, that Jonah actually died there. High weeds of the sea were all about his head. But the fish took him aboard and then threw him up on dry land just a few miles from where he had gotten on the ship. Jonah landed running toward Nineveh, and the revival came, and Nineveh repented. Jonah was God's man.

Listen to me, young people. Do you think you can run from Almighty God? You can run from God's blessing, but you can't run from God's judgment. You can run from God's appointment, and you can meet the hand of God in justice on your head; but you can't fool the Almighty. "Whither shall I go from thy spirit? or whither shall I flee from thy presence? If I ascend up into heaven, thou art there: if I make my bed in hell, behold, thou art there." You can't go anywhere and get away from God. How much it cost Jonah to learn that!

You remember the story of the sleepless king? He was king of the greatest empire of his day, and he couldn't sleep one night. He didn't know what was the matter. He tried a glass of wine, and that didn't make him drowsy. But he didn't send for his musicians. He said, "I know what will put me to sleep. I'll have them read the archives." Nothing is drier and more deadly and sleep inducing than old legal documents. So they wake up the men who keep the archives. Can't you see them now? Waked out of sleep, these old scholars rub their eyes and slip into their robes and put their conical hats on their heads and their spectacles on their noses and take up a lamp and go into the library to drag out something. They don't even know what they are getting. They just reach in and grab. They came to the king and began to read, droning it out. The king is not listening, but he is not asleep either. But he hears one thing that makes him wake up. There was a man who discovered a plot against the king's life, and the king had been informed of those plotters. They were taken and executed, and the king was spared.

The king said, "Wait a minute. Is there no record of any reward for this man who exposed the plot?" "No, there was no reward." Just then (for by now it is dawn, and the color of the sky is slipping in through the windows) a man comes to see him, the first arrival of the morning. He had already built a gallows on which he intended to hang this man who had exposed the plot. He hated him, for he was a Jew. The king greeted this man, Haman, with the words "What shall be done unto the man whom the king delighteth to honour?" And this egotistical old idiot thinks the king means him. He thought what he would like to have in the way of honor and said, "I'll tell you what to do. Get the best of the king's stallions out of the stable and put fine accoutrements on—saddles and bridles—and let an important nobleman lead that horse through the street and proclaim, 'Thus shall be done to the man whom the king delighteth to honour.' "

The king said, "That's fine. You go get Mordecai and put those robes on him and put him on that horse, and you lead him through the streets crying, 'Thus shall be done to the man whom the king delighteth to honour.' " And before the story is over, Haman hangs high on the gallows he had made for Mordecai; and his plot to destroy all the Jews in the land is frustrated by Esther, who is a Jewish queen.

God's plan is not going to be turned aside. Hitler tried it. He tried to get rid of all the Jews, but he didn't succeed. No man is going to turn aside a blessing when God has promised it. Herod was going to get rid of the baby Jesus. He said, "You go down there to Bethlehem, and you kill all the young boys, every one of them." There was a great cry that went up as the babies were all slain, but he didn't get the baby Jesus. He was playing in the warm sands under the palm trees of Egypt, for God had sent an angel to Joseph to say, "You take the babe and His mother and go down to Egypt." God always follows through.

It is interesting also how unpredictable God's instruments are. I look at you who are sitting here and wonder, "What does the Lord have for that person? What is the future for that girl?" You know, I have seen God use some mighty unlikely people. He has a way of using the instruments of His choosing. His ways are not our ways. His thoughts are not our thoughts. You may sit here as the most unlikely freshman in Bob Jones University; but if the Lord tarries, God may use you on a mission field somewhere. You may be used of God to hold back His wrath from a people as you preach the gospel and bring people to Christ. What can you do?

Men looked one time at a man who was the fastest base runner in the game of baseball. They cheered that man as a great baseball player, but God didn't see the baseball player. God saw Billy Sunday, the great evangelist. There was a man who went out selling shoes. He was a good shoe salesman and got big orders, but God saw a man who was to be a bigger man than a shoe salesman. God saw Dwight Moody, who was to preach in Europe and America and bring almost a whole generation to God. You can be what God wants you to be. It's a wonderful thing to be God's servant in God's place.

Who would ever have thought Saul of Tarsus would be the greatest missionary and the greatest writer of Scripture of any man in all the world and through all the ages? There he was, on the road to Damascus, ready to deliver God's people over for suffering and martyrdom. God spoke to him on the road to Damascus, and he was smitten from his horse and blinded. He went on to Damascus led by the hand, and there a man came to him who had been sent by God. Paul heard a voice. "Saul, Saul, why persecutest thou me?" And he replied, "Who art thou, Lord?" "I am Jesus whom thou persecutest: it is hard for thee to kick against the pricks." And this man who hated Jesus became a martyr for Jesus; but before his head rolled, he wrote the epistles and founded churches. Wherever he went, he spoke of that experience on a Damascus road that changed his life. Who would ever have thought the greatest enemy of God's people would become a martyr for God and a missionary for the Savior whom he hated?

You remember the story of David, don't you? Interesting little story, a story children like but that thrills adults too. Here is a great giant who comes out blaspheming God and threatening the people of Israel. There is a whole army there, and nobody is doing anything about it. Nobody has flung a javelin. Nobody has let fly an arrow. Everybody is cowering behind the bulwarks of the camp, and little David goes out—not in armor, not in mighty accoutrements, but with a slingshot and a pebble. He lets the pebble fly, and it stuns the giant; and with the giant's own sword, he cuts off his head. That puts a little courage into the faint hearts of the people of God, and they go out and mop up the operations and have victory. Who would ever have thought a sling would overcome an army? God's instrument.

Out in the desert there is a bush that burns and is not consumed, and it attracts the attention of a man who is keeping sheep. The voice of God speaks out of that bush, and Moses is called to go out and serve God. Who would ever have thought a burning bush in the desert could be the means of God's attracting the heart and attention of a man whom God needed?

Jezebel is still alive. Ahab is dead, and God sends Jehu to get rid of the whole line. Wouldn't you have thought this mighty man, this captain, could have handled that woman? He didn't need to. He just looked up at the window where she was. She had painted her face and was trying to attract him—an old hag now trying to look like a young, attractive woman; and he said to the men who looked after her (the eunuchs who took care of her dressing and her jewels), "Throw her down." And those half-men threw down the great queen. The dogs devoured her flesh and lapped her blood. They didn't touch the dirty palms of her hands or the soles of her feet that had gone so many times on errands of mischief.

It wasn't lightning that God used to destroy a presumptuous king who presumed to offer incense in the temple where God had forbidden any but the priests to offer the incense. God just sent a little leprosy, and the man never left the temple area until the day he died but was confined in a little outhouse—a king whom God stopped with leprosy.

It didn't take an earthquake and a fire to bring Jericho down. All it took were a few blasts from trumpets and some marching orders carried out as they paraded around the town. God doesn't need atomic power to do His will. God can use the prayers of the saints to shake down the strongholds of the Devil. It didn't take a great army to win a victory. All it took were three hundred men with some lamps hidden in pitchers and trumpets. And they blew the trumpets and broke the pitchers and let the light shine. The enemy thought, "Boy, there is a great crowd that has come after us"; and they began to kill each other in the dark. You don't need mighty forces. All you need is the power of the Holy Spirit in your life and the grace of God.

Down in southeast Alabama where my dad grew up, there was a community atheist. (In every little town or community there usually is somebody who thinks he is bigger than God and who blasphemes.) This man hated God, and he hated everybody else except one little girl. He had a little daughter about three or four years old, and she was the idol of his eye. There was a hollow tree outside the house where the child used to go and play house. One day when she was there a sudden thunderstorm came up—only one flash of lightning, but it hit the tree and killed the child. The man was frantic. He was furious. He cursed God and shook his fist in the face of the Almighty and said, "Why don't you match your strength against a man? Why pick on a little child?" He took the little girl in his arms and carried her in the house. The neighbor ladies came in to wash the child and prepare her for burial. They couldn't stand the man's cursings and blasphemies, so they said, "You go out and cut some wood and let's heat some water." He went out and picked up an axe; and under the axe handle, God had put a little microscopic insect, and it bit him on the hand. Within twenty-four hours he was dead of gangrene. God didn't need lightning to get rid of one blaspheming infidel. All He needed was a little insect in the woodpile. God's instruments are unpredictable.

God's judgments are inescapable. You can't miss God's judgment. God's judgment is as certain as God's righteousness, and those who reject God's grace and refuse God's purpose must face God's judgment. Men may go through life and boast of the fact that they don't fear God and don't need God and that they are not afraid of anything, but let's go to the judgment. What a picture that is. Those who are there have come from all the ancient graves where the ungodly dead have lain. They have come from old mausoleums. Some have come up from the ocean where they have lain through these centuries. They stand now in the presence of God and look out of eyes that worms have long ago eaten, and now they behold the wonder of God's creation. They look on Him who sits on the throne. And what do they do? They cry out for the rocks to fall on them. They want the old graves again and the drowning waves— anything is better than the eye of God. Listen, you have to face God sometime. You have to face Him in life, or you face Him in judgment; but you can't escape Him. He's the inescapable figure of all the ages. Every man has to meet Jesus sometime—at the cross or in the judgment, in the joy He can bring to a life or in the tragedy of a life lived without Him. But His judgment is inescapable.

If I had to stop here, I would quit preaching. His mercy is unlimited. I don't mean by that that a man can continue to sin against God and reject His grace. There is a verse in the Bible that we oftentimes disregard. "Seek ye the Lord while he may be found, call ye upon him while he is near." That means there is going to be a time when you can't find Him and a day when He is afar off. You have to find God in God's time and God's place. God says, "My spirit will not always strive with man." It is only as God's Holy Spirit strives with sinful hearts that sinful hearts are moved to turn to God. It is a terrible thing to reject the wooing of God's Spirit and to say no in the hour of God's conviction. For when a man no longer listens to the voice of God, one day God is going to withdraw that voice. The Holy Spirit is a sensitive person—the most sensitive person in all the universe. He can finally come to the place where

He is grieved and departs forever; and when He departs, He never comes back again. There are people in this town who may live here twenty-five or fifty years yet, but they are as damned as if they were already in hell because they have sinned away that day of grace, and God's Spirit has departed. No man knows when that hour comes; but when God's Holy Spirit leaves, man's judgment is settled forever.

But His mercy is unlimited. He can save to the uttermost all who come to God by Him. Whatever the past is, whatever the rebellion has been, whatever may be the nature of the sins, He can forgive them. There is power in the blood. There is mercy with the Lord, and "as many as received him, to them gave he power to become the sons of God, even to them that believe on his name." God may have brought you here for this night, for this time, for this opportunity. Grasp the opportunities that come. When the opportunity is gone, it never comes back again.

The Disobedient Prophet
I Kings 13

In the Bible there is an incident set down in the thirteenth chapter of I Kings. I call your attention to that chapter. This incident is very necessary and very applicable in our day because it teaches us some things we need to know. It clarifies some problems and confusion in the minds of God's people, and it teaches us a striking lesson on the matter of obedience.

Let us lay the background for the chapter. King Solomon died. Rehoboam, his son, came to the throne. Rehoboam was a very foolish, silly young man. He surrounded himself with young counselors as ignorant as he was. He was determined to outshine his father in magnificence.

The people came to him and said, "Your Majesty, your father taxed us heavily to build the temple and the palaces, but now Jerusalem is a beautiful city. We cannot stand this excess taxation. Please lighten the tax load." He conferred with his young counselors and sent back this message to the people: "My father whipped you with ropes, but I will whip you with scorpions." He increased the taxes. The result was that a revolution broke out. No nation can stand excess taxation over a long period of time without either bankruptcy or revolution.

The revolution was led by a man named Jeroboam. God had made it clear that because of Solomon's sin and apostasy, the kingdom was going to be divided; and so it was. Jeroboam was victorious. He took off the northern tribes, and they established the kingdom of Samaria. Now this man, having established his own kingdom with his capital in Samaria, was wise enough to realize that if he did not sever the religious tie that bound his people to their brethren in the south, he would soon lose his kingdom, for they would be reunited with the people in Jerusalem. So he established places of worship in his own kingdom. He built altars and set up calves, like the golden calf that was set up in the wilderness. He said to his people, "I want to make it easy for you to serve God." You beware of any man who is going to make it easy for you to serve God. It is never easy to serve God. Salvation is free, but service is costly. It always costs you something if you are worth anything to God. Jeroboam ordained priests, the offscouring of the earth. No good man who was of the tribe of Levi would be a priest of paganism and apostasy, so he had to get the worst kind of people he could. He had established his altar in Samaria and was dedicating the altar when the chapter opens.

There appeared on the scene a man of God, apparently a young man. He was nameless and was known only as God's man. He came up from Judah in the south and made the journey up to the capital of the new kingdom of Israel, where he stood before the altar where the king was burning incense and dedicating this apostasy, and he cried out according to the Word of the Lord. No preacher had any right to cry except according to the Word of the Lord. He said in effect, "The bones of those who make sacrifice will be burned upon your altar. You may know, O king, that I speak the truth. This altar is going to break asunder, and the ashes are going to pour out on the ground."

The king, interrupted in his apostasy, pointed to God's man and said, "Seize that fellow." As the soldiers seized God's man, the king found he was paralyzed and could not draw back his pointing finger. He stood there like a scarecrow with his hand pointing out, but he said to God's man, "Intercede with God that my arm may be restored." Strange thing. God's enemies, when they get in trouble, want God's man to pray for them. They do not go to somebody who has no more power with God than they do, but they come to God's man and ask for prayer. And God's man prayed for this king, and his arm was restored to its usefulness.

Bear in mind that this was not done for the king's sake. It was done for the sake of God's man. God said, "By hearing that prayer,

I want you to know, apostate king, that this is My servant, and he has some influence with the court of heaven. Because he asks it, I will do it." This king is not repentant. He is merely frustrated. There is much that passes in our day for repentance that is frustration. We have had from time to time some student whose life was not right. He knew he was going to be caught in something he had been doing that was wrong, so he would come in and stage a repentance and pretend to be saved, hoping thereby to escape the expulsion he had earned for himself. That is not genuine. That is frustration. You see, repentance is grief over sin. Frustration is grief in being caught in your sin and not getting by with it. Do not ever deceive yourself, young people. True repentance brings God's forgiveness, but frustration is not repentance. This king continued his apostasy, and at the end of the chapter he was still ordaining these ungodly priests.

Now that his arm is restored, King Jeroboam said, "You go back to the palace. I want to give you a reward. Have breakfast with me, and have a reward for what you have done." This prophet is not like one of these Charismatic radio preachers with his hand outstretched every time he brings to pass some phony miracle. This is a genuine miracle and a genuine man of God. He said, "I do not want your reward. God told me not to eat bread or drink water in this place. I cannot sit down at your table. This is a land of apostasy. I am going to have nothing to do with it. God told me not to take anything." He turned his back on the king and started south toward Judah.

Now let's go to the house of a man who lives nearby. He, too, is God's man. He, too, is a prophet; and he, too, is nameless. He is known as the old prophet, or the prophet of Bethel. An old man, God's man; and here he is. This old man is not one who goes along with the apostasy. He has not had a share in the idolatry. He stayed home, very carefully holding himself aloof from it. But this man is a perfect picture of the New Evangelical. He should have gone to cry out against this apostasy. Is it not a tragic situation that God has to send a man all of the way from Judah to do a job that a prophet in the shadow of the sin is not doing? He should have been there crying out against this altar. I am sure he had a good excuse for not going. Maybe he said, "You know, if I go up there and cry out

17

against what the king is doing, he will cut my head off; and I am the only prophet left in this land, the only true prophet of God. Better a live prophet with his mouth shut than a dead prophet with his mouth open." Whoever told you such a thing as that? A dead prophet with his head cut off because of his open speech in defense of God's truth is worth more to God than a hundred prophets hiding by fifties in the caves and being fed from the table of Ahab.

Oh, he had a good excuse. He was taking care of himself. You know, there is many a man today who will not stand up and be counted on God's side in this day of compromise and unbelief and New Evangelicalism because he is afraid for himself. He looks forward to the time when he will begin to get his denominational pension, or he looks forward to the church he hopes to gain; and he knows no man is ever popular who stands alone and cries out against that which is going on. But it is significant his sons had gone. You show me a man who compromises God's truth, and I will show you a man whose sons have no respect for God's truth. And I daresay his sons became priests of the apostasy. The sons came back and said to the old man, "You should have been there." Well, he should have been there to oppose it. Look, it is all right to go to an ecumenical meeting if you go there to march up and down outside with a placard saying, "This is of the Devil. This is not of God." It is all right to go and hand out tracts condemning the apostasy and the unbelief. That is all right. But if you go and sit in the place, they will count you as one of them. In fact, they will count you as ten of that crowd. That is about the way they exaggerate the figures of this apostasy today.

Well, the boys said, "You should have gone," and they told the old man what happened. He said, "Which way did that fellow go?" Is it not strange that an old compromiser, an old man who has no character himself, no backbone and no intestinal fortitude, is concerned to meet a man who is more courageous than he is? The boys said, "He took such-and-such a road." "All right," said the old man, "saddle me the ass." They brought the donkey around, and he climbed into the saddle.

Unfortunately, he overtook God's man, who was seated under a tree. Always when you find in the Old Testament a prophet under a tree, he is in the place of defeat. God has no time for us to sit in the shade until the job is done and the battle is finished. The shade comes at even, after the battle is over and the sword is wet with blood and the bruises of the battle burn upon your flesh. But he sat there under the tree feeling sorry for himself. The old prophet rode up and looked over his spectacles between the ears of his donkey and said, "Are you that man of God?"

"Yea, I am God's man."

"Well, I want you to come to my house and have some fellowship, and we will have a meal together."

"I cannot do it. God told me when I came here to eat no bread and drink no water in this place."

"Oh, it is all right for you to go to my house. You see, God sent an angel to me to tell you He had changed His mind about that. I am a prophet too, and it is all right for you to fellowship with me." But, says the Scripture, the old prophet lied to him. You beware of the cowards and the compromisers and the New Evangelicals. They will always lie. Either they will lie about what they are doing to make it seem less bad, or they will lie about you and impugn your motives because you stand against their compromise. But God's man fell for it; and he got on his donkey, and the four asses went back to the old prophet's house—two riding and two walking. A disobedient prophet is a fool indeed.

They got to the old prophet's house and had a meal together; and in the midst of the meal, the old prophet was suddenly taken by God's Spirit. God spoke through the mouth that had lied, and He spoke judgment. "Because you came back and ate and drank where I told you not to eat and drink, you will never sleep with your fathers." That is not much of a curse to a twentieth-century Gentile, but it was to an Old Testament Jew. To be buried in the family sepulchre was the sign of an honorable life. You read in the Scripture, "He was gathered to his fathers"; "He slept with his fathers." They had a family sepulchre and a stone over the door.

When a man died, they washed the body, wrapped it in a sheet, and took it the same day he died into the sepulchre and sealed it again. The dust of the generations was mingled in the family sepulchre.

I do not know who this man's ancestors were, but they must have been godly people for because of one act of disobedience, he lost the right to lie in the tomb with them. The meal being over, with a full stomach and a heavy heart, he started again toward Judah. We come now to the text in the twenty-fourth verse—one little phrase of that verse. "A lion met him by the way, and slew him." Out of the hills came a mountain lion. This country was filled with wild beasts at that time. He struck the man from the donkey and slew him. The lion did not attack the poor donkey. Both the lion and the ass stood there, and people passed by and saw the prophet's carcass and reported it in the town where the old prophet dwelt. You know what he said? He didn't say, "That is the man I lied to and helped destroy." Oh, no. Such a person never takes responsibility. He said, "I know who that is. That is the man who disobeyed God. He ate and drank where God told him not to eat and drink." He then goes and drives off the lion and takes the man's body and buries it in his own sepulchre, right up above the valley where this altar of apostasy had been set.

This is a tragic story. Here is a man who in the dawn came out with God's message, crowned with the very power and glory of God. There is no higher privilege than to be God's man, God's ambassador, God's spokesman. Sunrise found him declaring God's counsel, refusing a king's reward, working miracles in prayer. Midmorning found him seated under a tree, deceived. High noon found him eating and drinking in disobedience to God. The first star of evening came out as they buried him in the tomb of the man who lied to him. That is the outline of the story. Let us look at it now for a few moments in detail.

That this is God's man there can be no doubt. He came there, especially appointed of God, to do a job; and God gave him a threefold command. Note this command carefully because it is set forth in three simple commands that contain everything the Bible has to tell us about how God's men ought to deal with apostasy. It sums up here in three simple fragments of one command all that we need to know about apostasy and how it should be dealt with. Some of you students have been asking us questions about apostasy. What is it? How may I know it? How may I recognize it?

Apostasy is not error. Error is due to ignorance of God's Word. You study the Word of God carefully and you will be kept from error. Apostasy is not heresy. Heresy is a cancer on the body of faith. A cancer destroys the body because cells become abnormal and grow until they suck out and destroy the life of wholesome cells. Heresy is religious cancer. Every heresy is based upon some good Bible doctrine which has become abnormal in our thinking, and we have not balanced it off with a study of the Word of God, that sets forth other points which would keep us in balance. Heresies all have their foundation in good doctrine. The Charismatic heresy is based upon a false interpretation and a wild interpretation of the Bible's teaching on the doctrine of the Holy Spirit. Every heresy is founded upon some good doctrine, but it is a doctrine which has grown abnormal and unwholesome. The Holy Spirit can free men from heresy; but apostasy is a deliberate turning away, a falling away, a rejection, an opposition to God's truth. There is no remedy for apostasy, but God sends judgment.

We are living in a day when there is much heresy—false religions, cults; but we are living in a day when the great standard of our day is the standard of apostasy. There are efforts to get all kinds of people—those in the World Council of Churches, the Roman Catholic Church, etc.—into one great super church, one great organization. When that is done, we will have the church of Antichrist, not the church of Christ. You cannot at the same time have both ecumenicity and obedience to the Word of God, for God commands us that we must come out and touch not the unclean thing. There is nothing as unclean in the Word of God as apostasy. Apostasy is always associated with adultery, uncleanness, immorality. Wherever apostasy abounds, the lusts of the flesh abound. It is not to be surprising to us that today immorality has grown apace with the unbelief and apostasy in the ecclesiastical body and in the churches (so-called) of Jesus Christ.

Now, this young man was told to do three things. First, he was
sent to denounce this apostasy, this false religion, this deliberate
rejection of God's truth, this turning away from God's commands.
God decreed that those who worship Him must worship Him in
spirit and in truth and that the place of worship must be the temple
there in Jerusalem. This king had said, "I do not want you to have
to make the journey there. It is too far to go in bad weather with
your little children and your families. You can serve God here."
But, my friend, God has a will about where you worship as well as
how you worship. You have no more business staying in some
apostate denomination affiliated with the World Council than you
have in going out and sacrificing some beast on an altar somewhere
in the hills. God has a will about where you worship. The commands
are quite clear. When the temple was built, there were to be no more
mountain altars, no more groves and high places. The only place
an acceptable sacrifice could be made to God was in the temple at
Jerusalem. That temple stands there as a part of the same mountain
range on which Mount Calvary rests. God willed that the sacrifices
be made on this mountain where the Lord Jesus was to die for our
sins. "You go there, and you cry out against apostasy."

I had an interesting letter from a graduate today. It was a letter
that disturbed me a little and troubled me because I thought a
graduate would know better. He is a man who has been out many
years. He said, "Dr. Bob, I am a pastor of an independent church,
as you know. I have been approached by an organization that wants
to get independent churches together under sort of an umbrella, a
covering. Do you know anything about the organization?" I must
confess that I had never heard of it. This graduate said, however,
that there were three things in their literature that troubled him. In
the first place, there was no doctrinal statement, no clear declaration
of what they believed. In the second place, they spoke well of the
word "ecumenicity" and declared that they were ecumenical. In the
third place, they quoted a well-known "liberal," a well-known
unbeliever; and they quoted him in the literature with approval. I
wrote this graduate back and said, "You should not have to ask me
that. Any organization that will not declare what they believe does

not believe right." Bob Jones University is glad to say what we believe. We announce it here every day when we gather and say our creed together. We do not hide in our literature what we believe about the Word of God. We believe that "all Scripture is given by inspiration of God," that everything this Book says is so. You will not find any unbeliever quoted with approval from this platform. We think ecumenicity is the work of the Devil and is condemned in the Word of God. Nobody should be affiliated with it.

"You go there and cry out against it." No man has the right to speak well of unbelievers and apostates. You should condemn them vigorously. Do you know, if anybody stood in a pulpit and used the same language toward these modern apostates that the Lord used to the religious apostates of His day, we would be accused of being unloving and unkind. He said to those religious hypocrites, "You are whited sepulchres full of dead men's bones. You are dirty pitchers on the inside. You try to look nice on the outside. You will not go into the door of salvation yourself, and you keep others from going in." My, how He spoke of them. But what He said of them is the same kind of thing we must say of unbelievers and apostates.

Sometimes an evangelist will get up when he has these ecumenical crusades, with apostates and unbelievers and cultists on his platform, and will speak well of them and call them men of God. My friend, they are not children of God. They are children of the Devil and servants of Satan. Call them what they are. "You go there and denounce this apostasy." That is the first part of the command. Do not try to make up to them. Do not try, as the New Evangelicals do, to find some bridge by which you can reach them. Condemn them. Speak out against them. Call down God's judgment upon them, for God says His judgment will be upon them. God says it is impossible to renew them to repentance. For them are reserved the mists of blackness forever. You call apostates what they are. They are men who once knew the truth but who have departed from the truth. They have fallen away, and they have fallen away under God's judgment.

The second part of the command was, "You are not to eat bread or drink water in that place." Why? Because you are not to be obligated to apostasy for any reward. If you are a preacher in a denomination that is apostate, you will have to depend upon the denominational secretary, who is a part of a machine, to recommend you for a church; or there will be some bishop or district superintendent who will get you a church. You knuckle under. You serve those who pay your salary, or you are out on your ear. "You do not take so much as a crust of bread or a glass of water from this land that is in the grip of apostasy. You have gone there to condemn the apostasy, to warn the people against it, to cry 'Repent' against this sort of thing. Don't let them give you any reward, no matter what happens."

The third part of the command is "Get out of it. Get out as quickly as you can. Having denounced it, having rejected its rewards, turn your back on it and scamper for home. Come home by another road. Do not take that regular road that goes through the valley. Hurry up over the hills through that goat path where you can get out quickly and reach the border. You have no business staying in apostasy."

Well, he did the first part. He denounced the apostasy. He did it well. He refused the reward—for a time—but did not get out of it. He stopped on the way home. Sitting under that tree, he felt sorry for himself. "You know, they say the laborer is worthy of his hire. The Lord knows I have not had a cup of coffee yet. I got up before day to get up here. I did not take the reward. Boy, you know, we had a good meeting too—a real healing meeting. Oral Roberts could not have done better. We had a good time. That old king's arm was stiff. The Lord healed him. Is not that wonderful? Boy, I put on a good program up there. I did what the Lord told me to do." But he is not across the border yet. If he had gone a little further and settled down beyond the border, that older compromiser could not have overtaken him and brought him back.

As long as you stay within the entanglements of that which God condemned, you put yourself in the way of being trapped and bound and deceived. Get out of it. If there is anybody here today who is still in a church that is affiliated with the National Council of Churches—that is in the grip of apostasy and unbelief, that supports seminaries that deny the Word of God, that has pastors who will support that which God condemns—you had better get out of it. God will judge you if you stay in. God called the apostasy and the ecumenical movement a cage of dirty birds. He said, "I am going to wring some necks sometime." If you are in that cage, you will get your neck wrung and your feathers plucked when the judgment comes on it. Get out of it lest you fall into her judgments and are judged with her.

The young man did everything except get across the border. He was deceived, but he is responsible for his own deception. He had not obeyed to the nth degree. He had gone so far and given out of spiritual and moral wind. There are folks here like that. You have done this, and you have done that, and you have done the other; but you have held back. You have not done it all. You have never stepped out by complete faith in obedience to God if you have tried somehow to leave yourself a little avenue of escape if it gets so tight that you can run back to the Devil's crowd for help and have tried to keep your alliances.

We have had students in Bob Jones University who figured, "I will graduate from Bob Jones University so I will learn how to preach and how to do the job; then I will go to the Convention seminary, my denominational theological school, to get their imprimatur upon me so I can get a church." If you are in that fix, you are just like this young man. You have not quite cut loose.

This young man was deceived, but he was responsible for his deception. He had not obeyed God fully. He was responsible for his own deception because he listened to a man who talked of angels when he had the Word of God. As long as you have God's Word, if you are deceived, there is nobody to blame but you. This old man did not talk about God. He talked about an angel. He was not so far gone that he dared to lie about God, so he blamed it on an angel. It is not quite so heinous and blasphemous. I meet people who talk to angels—but never but once; and I run as far as I can to the nearest exit. A fellow told me once, "Well, Bob, I had an angel talk to me last night."

I said, "Whoa, how do you know it was an angel?"

"It looked like an angel."

"What does an angel look like?"

"An angel looks like that thing that was talking to me."

That is all the sense they have. This sounds just like a typical Charismatic. I said, "It might have been the Devil, if it was not indigestion."

He said, "Do not be blasphemous."

I said, "I am being scriptural. The Bible says the Devil can transform himself into an angel of light. If something comes by your bedside and tells you something, before you do what he tells you, you had better get up and look at God's Word. If what he told you is contrary to God's Word, you know where he came from. He did not come from heaven." And the Devil can transform himself into an angel of light. I do not care who the man is, how prominent he is, how well known he is, or whether he has preached in Moscow or not. If he tells you something contrary to God's Word and you believe him when you have God's Word, you are responsible for God's judgment that comes upon you.

He listened, and he was deceived, and he was destroyed. You say, "Wait a minute. Was not God hard on that fellow? All he did was have a meal with a brother who lied to him. Do you not think God was pretty harsh to kill him?" What do you think about it? Not that it makes any difference. The issue is who is God? What is God? Is He sovereign? All of the integrity of deity was at stake in this matter. He had said to that king and to those people, "God is going to judge your apostasy, and God has judged this kingdom. God told me not even to take so much as a piece of bread and a glass of water here." If the word got back that he disobeyed God's command and ate and drank and went unpunished, do you not think the king would say, "God must not mean what He says"?

You know, a man's life can negate everything he says from the pulpit. There is many a preacher who preaches well but lives very badly. What you live in your life is just as important as what you say in the pulpit or in public. If your life is not in conformity to the Word of God you preach, then you had better quit preaching. If this man got by with his disobedience, what about all of those weak people halting between two opinions, whether to serve the king's apostasy or to believe God and turn in repentance to the Word of God? You know, God sometimes has to punish a disobedient godly man for the sake of the ungodly. In the book of Corinthians we are told how, because of sin, some are sick and some have even died (fallen asleep). God sometimes has to take a man home early because that man's life is a reproach and a rebuke to the ministry of the Word of God. You had better not try to disobey God and hope to get by with it. You cannot do it.

There were three men I knew as a young man, all good preachers and all outstanding. One was possibly one of the best-known and most glib Bible teachers we ever had in America. He once asked me, "Why do you not have me come speak at Bob Jones University?" I had to say to him, "Because I do not want your influence on our students." He would interpret Scripture one way one day; and the next time he was on the air, he would contradict what he had said before. He was a very inconsistent man. He was a man who stood for the Word of God, but he became involved. In order to get a national radio program on the network, he knuckled under to the National Council of Churches. He was not on the air under that sponsorship very long until he died of a brain tumor.

At the same time, there was a young man who had radio programs and a great ministry to youth. He began to criticize those who would not go along with ecumenical evangelism. He said they were unloving and were the enemies of the gospel and were not concerned about the salvation of souls. This man, though he professed to believe the Bible, set himself up against those who were trying to obey the Bible. It was not many weeks until he died, still a young man.

Another man used to be here on our Bible Conference program. He was a tremendous preacher—a man with great ability who took a strong stand against apostasy and condemned denominational apostasy. As he got older, he found he was not getting as many invitations to conferences as he had been; so he aligned himself with the Southern Baptist Convention, which he had condemned most vigorously before. He put his sons in Southern Baptist institutions. Within a few months his funeral was held from the chapel of Baylor University in Texas. I do not say that God killed these men because they had tarnished their testimony and betrayed the truth they had preached; but I say it is a very interesting coincidence, at least, that each of these men, when he departed from the thing he had held to and began to condemn those who would not follow his bad example, was taken out of the world. It is a tragic thing to see a man's ministry destroyed because of his disobedience.

A lion came and got the prophet. What a tragedy that was. That was the end of the life and ministry of this man. I wonder not only who he was but what he might have been if he had obeyed God. He listened to men when he had God's clear-cut command. You can easily be swayed if you are not armed and alert and involved in the Word of God.

I have preached to Christians tonight. If you are here without salvation, how do you expect to escape when you neglect God's offer of salvation? If it is necessary for God to destroy a disobedient child to preserve His integrity and save those who are being betrayed by his betrayal, do you think God can let you escape when you refuse His grace? If you are still God's enemy, rejecting His Son and refusing Him, there is a worse lion ahead of you than got this man. His teeth are sharp. His claws are poisonous. His breath is fetid. A lion lies across the path of every sinner, and the name of that lion is hell, for the wicked shall be turned into hell. Here is a man who obeyed part of the way but did not obey all. A lion met him by the way and slew him.

There are folks here tonight who are still in disobedience to God. You are making allowances for the flesh to fulfill the lusts thereof. You are ambitious for the approval of the ungodly. You desire to be thought well of by those who do not think well of your Savior. There are some of you who have given God everything except one or two things. You have surrendered everything except your passion or your ambitions or your desire for something in life. You are in disobedience. This applies not only in relationship to apostasy but also to every aspect of your life. No man has obeyed who has not obeyed wholly, and no man is surrendered who has not surrendered all.

I wonder who here tonight is going to say, "God knows there are things in my life that are not surrendered yet. There is disobedience that I have regarded lightly. But I want to come clean tonight. I want to be all out for the Lord. I want to be known as God's man or woman whatever it costs, be it life, reputation, what the world considers joy, or whatever it is. I do not want it if it is going to keep me from knowing God's smile of approval and the full ministry that God has for me." I know this is not easy. I am not trying to make it easy for you to serve God. The lines need to be drawn. Jesus never makes it easy. He said, "If you will come after me, you will have to deny yourself." You have to take up a cross daily and follow. I will not try to tell you that something is easy which the Lord says is hard.

Let us pray. Our Father, we thank Thee for those who have come. May no one leave this place with anything between him and his Lord, with any unsurrendered corner, any inch of ground that has not been claimed by the Lord Jesus and over which He does not rule. We pray it in His name. Amen.

.

The Harvest Is Past

Jeremiah 8:20

I would suggest that you do not turn to the text tonight. It is a brief sentence, and you can read it for yourself if you wish when you get home; but I will be into the sermon before you find the text. It is Jeremiah 8:20—"The harvest is past, the summer is ended, and we are not saved."

"We are not saved." You can hear the cries of the dying and the groans of the damned and the shrieks of the lost in that text. "We are not saved." What a terrible thing it is not to be saved. "We are not saved," and salvation is so important. If you can judge a thing by its price, then salvation is the most precious thing under God's sky, for we are purchased not with silver and gold but with the precious blood of the Lord Jesus Christ.

Our salvation depends upon His sacrifice, the fact that He gave Himself a ransom for us. What a waste it is, the blood of Christ, to those who will not accept Him. He went to a cross. He suffered all the anguish of all the damned forever in hell. He cried in that prophetic passage, "The pains of hell gat hold upon me." How He, the infinite Son of God, could suffer in those brief hours on the cross all the anguish of all the lost of all the generations in hell forever I cannot explain. I cannot explain that any more than I can explain the love of Christ, but our sins sent Him to the cross to die for us.

But in that hour of anguish he suffered not just the anguish of the body but the pains of all the lost men in eternity forever, and *such* a price was paid; yet "we are not saved." What a waste that is—to see a man in eternity in the flames of hell and know he does not have to be there, for Jesus Christ has already borne in His own body all the penalty that man will endure forever among the lost.

What a terrible thing that is. "We are not saved," and salvation is so important.

I was listening to the news before I came over tonight telling of the hijacking of that plane there in Karachi and how finally, when the lights went out, the hijackers panicked and began to shoot and cast grenades. Some fifteen or sixteen people were killed and over one hundred were injured. Two of the hijackers were shot, and the other three were captured. I thought, "What a terrible thing that is, how sudden, how unexpected." When those people boarded that plane in New York, they thought they would be in Frankfurt in a few hours. But where are they now? They are in eternity.

And one thing is dead sure as you read the Word of God. Whatever decision a man or woman makes for eternity must be made in time, for after death comes the judgment. You cannot change your destiny when life is gone and the soul has left the body. "We are not saved." How uncertain life is. I am sure most of you here have had a chance to be saved, and most of you are saved; but tonight I may be talking to somebody who grew up in a Christian home. The first word your mother whispered in your baby ear after birth was the name of Jesus. The first thing you learned to recite was "Now I lay me down to sleep. I pray Thee, Lord, my soul to keep." You grew up in a house of faith with concerned parents who pointed you to Jesus. Maybe you went to a church where they had an old-fashioned preacher who preached the gospel and spoke of life and death, of heaven and hell, of decisions to be made, and of the blood of Jesus Christ.

But all this has not done you any good unless you have believed unto life. All the virtues of a godly parent cannot redeem a son, though the example and the teaching can bring him to a knowledge of Jesus Christ. I believe if a child is brought up in "the way he should go . . . when he is old, he will not depart from it." But salvation is a personal and individual matter, and each man for himself must make the decision where his destiny shall be.

You may try to put it off. You may say, "Not now; some other time." Hell is full of people who put off the decision, who said, "I will settle it by and by. Don't bother me now. There are things I want to do and jobs I want to accomplish and places I want to go and achievements I intend to achieve." You have decided not to be bothered. You have had a chance to be saved.

You say, "Dr. Bob, you are not describing me. I did not grow up in a home like that." Maybe you are the only one in your family who even knows the gospel. You may say, "I did not go to a church where the truth was preached, where God's Word was opened. If I went to church at all, it was to an unbelieving church, a 'liberal' church with no gospel and no authority of the Word of God. I have never had a chance to be saved." Oh, yes, you have. You had a chance last night and the night before, and you have a chance tonight, for God says, "Behold, now is the accepted time; behold, now is the day of salvation."

But the chances are passing. All of life's opportunities go by on winged wheels. The old Greeks used to depict time as a man with a great forelock of hair, but the back of his head was bald. The picture is very plain. If I would grasp opportunity, I must seize it as it comes toward me because once opportunity has passed by, there is nothing I can lay hold of to draw it back again. So it is with the opportunities of life.

How quickly life goes by. How soon it is passed. Looking back over the years I have lived, life all merges together into sort of a shifting scene; but it all seems too short. Perhaps you have heard older people say, "You know, the older you grow, the faster time goes by." That is true, really. The years go by like the mileposts on a railroad outside the window of a speeding train. When they still had passenger trains and we took speedy journeys across the plains, you could sit and watch the mileposts go by.

I remember as a boy traveling across the country with my father, who was in evangelistic work. I would love to stand on the back platform of a train and watch the mileposts go by. That is the way the year goes by. It is New Year's, Easter, Thanksgiving, Christmas, and a year has gone by. That is the way life streams past. The strange thing is that the train gets faster on its journey, and every year the mileposts move more swiftly by.

What is man? He "is of few days, and full of trouble." A man who is not saved is not prepared for this life any more than he is prepared for the life that lies ahead beyond the grave.

You know, some people say—there is a great rash of this among young people today—"I am going to end my life. I am going to commit suicide." Oh, you poor fool. You cannot end your life. All you can do is transfer your existence from one place to another place because as long as God is on the throne, man must live somewhere forever. It is when angels sing funeral dirges over God's grave that you will cease to be, and that time will never come.

Sinners would be better off if they could end their life, go out into eternal nothingness, into one vast lengthy sleep; but, my friend, God has not made it that way. God has made it so that man has to live somewhere forever. There is not much choice. There are only two alternatives. There is hell or heaven; but, my, what a rich choice that is—to escape the fire and enjoy God's presence or to leave the place of regret, the prison house of eternity, and sit down at the table spread for those who love the Lord. Ah, there is all the difference in the world—and the opportunities pass by.

You know, the strange thing is that every time you resist the wooing of God's Spirit and refuse Jesus Christ's entrance into your heart, the more difficult it becomes the next time you have an opportunity—if you have an opportunity. Somehow the hinges grow rusty to the door of your heart, and the bolt becomes wedged in the socket. The best time you ever had to get saved was the first time you ever heard the gospel.

I knew a preacher once who said to me (he was a Jewish preacher who had been converted to Jesus Christ), "You know, I never refused the Lord. The first time I heard the gospel and realized that this was my Messiah, I trusted Him." It is easier the first time because you have not built resistance. "He, that being often reproved hardeneth his neck, shall suddenly be destroyed, and that without remedy."

One day the last chance will come. You will hear the gospel for the last time. God's Spirit will speak to you one final time. No man knows when that time arrives. There is many a man who has gone out of an evangelistic meeting rejecting the gospel and saying, "I will be saved another time," and there was no other time.

Years ago I dealt with a man in the inquiry room after a service. He said to me, "You know, we have an evangelistic campaign in this church every year. I have some things I need to look after this year, but next year in the evangelistic meeting, I am going to trust Jesus and be saved." That night he went out, and within twelve blocks of the church he was killed by a train at a crossing. Next year never came for him, for he passed from time into eternity a lost man.

How foolish it is to say, "Not now; some other time." You never know what tomorrow holds. No man knows what a day shall bring forth. You say, "Dr. Bob, are you trying to frighten us?" No, but if I could frighten you into the arms of Jesus, I would do it.

I was saved as a boy of five, and I was saved because I did not want to go to hell. I knew I was a sinner, and I trusted Jesus Christ; and all the fear of hell went away. I have never regretted the decision because I have been freed from the anguish and fear of eternal loss.

Did you ever stop to think what it must be like the first moment in hell? A man dies, sight fades, things grow dark around him, and he finds himself in hell. What must it be like in hell? No chance. No change. No relief. And for eternity there is anguish, there is regret over decisions that were not made and opportunities that were rejected.

But, my friend, you can live to be an old, old man or woman and be as lost for fifty years of your life as if you were already in hell. Years ago there was a Scottish preacher, a man named Guthrie, a very fine preacher. He was preaching in his old years in a little church in a highland village of Scotland. One night shortly before day, a woman with a lantern came knocking at the door of the house of the preacher for whom he was preaching, and this woman asked if the evangelist were there. When told that he was, she said, "Would you wake him? I need to talk to him." Dr. Guthrie dressed quickly and went down. The lady with the lantern said, "Look, there is a woman up in the highlands about five miles from here who is at the point of death. In fact, she has been in the anguish of death for three days. We did not know that you were here. Would you come up and talk to her?" Dr. Guthrie said, "Certainly, I will go."

He set out behind the woman with the lantern, and they went up into the highland country, climbing the rough hills and going through the heather. Eventually they came to a ridge just as the sun was beginning to give its first rays, though it had not appeared above the horizon. Down in the hollow at their feet there was a house, a typical Scotch peasant home built of fieldstone with a thatched roof and a great stone fireplace. There was a faint light as of from one candle coming through the windows.

They opened the door and went in, and as Dr. Guthrie entered, he could hear the sound of the dying rattle in the throat of a woman. There she was in the bed built into the wall at the end of the house, a bed with curtains around it. Two women were sitting by the fireplace which served not only to warm the room but also as a place for cooking.

Dr. Guthrie took the candle from the mantlepiece and put it on a shelf inside the bed where the light fell upon the woman. He began to talk to her. He dealt with the Psalms that the Scots love, and he quoted especially that Twenty-third Psalm. There was no sign of response. The woman's eyes were staring, and the rattle of death almost seemed to shake the house.

Finally, he leaned closer. He said, "Do you know I am talking to you? Are you conscious?"

For the first time the eyes seemed to fix upon his, and the woman said, "Yes, I know you. Your name is Guthrie. Years ago you were the minister in my parish. I was a young woman then. Every time you preached, God brought conviction of my need upon me; but I did not want to be bothered with God. I had other things I wanted to do. One day I said to God, 'I wish You would leave me alone.' He has left me alone; and from that day until this, God has not spoken to me. You can stand here and talk for an hour, but there is no hope for me; and I will be, in a few minutes in . . ." She was gone.

You cannot resist God save at your peril, and for more than fifty years this poor woman had been impervious to the gospel because God says His Spirit will not always strive with man; and when God's Spirit departs, there is no means of conviction in your life because the conviction comes from God. No wonder God says, "Seek ye the Lord while he may be found, call ye upon him while he is near." The chances are passing. Sometime the last chance is going to come. "We are not saved."

It is wonderful to be saved. It is wonderful in life. You who know Christ know the joy and the satisfaction you can have in Jesus Christ. I feel sorry for people who do not know Jesus. Where do they go in the hour of sorrow when a loved one dies? We go to the Lord Jesus. In the time of trouble, where do we seek relief? We seek it from the Word of God and the blessed Savior, the Shepherd who leads us in green pastures and who denies us no good thing. God's people have abundant joy.

There is a song in the heart of a Christian. Even in sorrow we sorrow not as others who have no hope. It is wonderful to be saved. You know, the world (unconverted people) think Christians must be awfully miserable. They like to go to church. They like to sing songs. They do not mind prayer meeting. They read their Bibles. What do they get out of life?

I will tell you what they get out of life—abundance of joy unspeakable and full of glory. Oh, they may not always be demonstrative; but inside there is a peace that passeth understanding, an assurance, a sweetness, a rest. You never find that save in the will of God.

It is wonderful in life to be saved. Have you ever seen a Christian bedridden, deformed, crippled, twisted, suffering, but with a smile of joy on the face, every day a day of new beginnings? I have known people like that. You go into their room, a simple room maybe in a little house somewhere; but you could feel God's presence when you got there. Though they could not move and could not even feed themselves, that place was light like the light of heaven because the Lord was there. You would go to try to comfort them, and you would go away with great comfort and great conviction in your own life as you contrasted your opportunities with theirs and were aware of your failures as they took advantage of every opportunity to testify for the Lord Jesus.

Listen, at best in this world, some in this place tonight are going to have hard lives. Disease will strike. Paralysis will come. There will be sudden death. With this many people, in the next few years some will not be here. Some will be in pain and anguish, some unfortunately married, unhappy, no joy as far as the world is concerned; but when you know Jesus Christ, there is peace inside and joy. It is wonderful in life to be saved. But the Lord does not save you just for heaven. He saves you for service and joy down here. He makes the world different. We sing a hymn sometimes about the sky's being richer blue and the world more vivid green since we came to know the Lord Jesus. That is not just poetic thought; that is truth.

It is wonderful in life to be saved, but it is wonderful in death to be saved. My dad used to tell in one of his sermons the story about a man who checked into the hotel in a small town; and he said to the desk clerk, "Don't send my bags up. I will take them up later." The man began to walk up and down the lobby. He would sit down and pick up the paper and put it down, move about, apparently miserable for some reason. Finally, the clerk came out from behind the desk and said, "Friend, you seem to be troubled. Is anything wrong? Is there anything I can do?"

He replied, "No, I was in that train wreck just before day out on the edge of town, and I cannot get the scenes out of my mind."

"Oh," said the clerk, "what happened?"

He said, "I don't know. I was sitting there half-asleep and felt the train on the ties. I knew we had jumped the track. The next thing I knew I was out in the field. I must have been thrown through the open window. I got up. I was just a bit stunned. I shook myself and went up to the track to see what I could do. It was the biggest mess you ever saw. Train cars were all piled up. It was difficult to realize it had ever been a train headed somewhere on a track. A fire had broken out in a coach up near the engine. The first person I came to was a lady—maybe fifty years, white-haired, sweet face—and she was lying there on her back. The train car was across her lower limbs, and I reached down to see if I could pull her out; but the whole weight of the car was upon her. I called some men nearby, and we got a pole and put it under the car and tried to pry it up; but the lady smiled sweetly and said, 'That is all right. You had better go help some of those other people.'

"I then became conscious of the cries and groans and shrieks, but I hated to leave that woman. She was such a sweet person, so I took off my coat and rolled it up and made kind of a pillow and lifted up her head and slipped it under to make her as comfortable as I could. She thanked me so sweetly, and for the next two hours we were carrying out the dead and the dying and the maimed. I heard somebody singing something about leaning on everlasting arms, and I noticed it was this lady pinned under the car. Every time I passed there, she was still singing; but the song grew weaker and more faint. Eventually I did not hear it anymore, and I went over and looked at her; and she was dead.

"Say," said the traveling man, "it must be wonderful in a time like that to have some everlasting arms to lean on." It is wonderful in death to be saved.

A woman gave birth to a beautiful baby and then began to slip away; and the doctor said to her, "I am afraid we are going to lose you. There is a door open, and you are going to go through that door." He was a Christian doctor. Thank God for Christian doctors. She said, "Is the door wide enough to take the baby?" He said, "No, the door is not wide enough to take the baby through; but the door is wide enough for Christ to go with you." It is wonderful in death to be saved.

But let us wait a minute. It is wonderful in eternity. You know, I do not know much about heaven. All I know about heaven is from the Bible, but the descriptions of heaven we get in the Book are generally about the eternal city that is going to come down from God out of heaven after this earth has been purged and cleansed and judged with fire. Not much is said about the place where the dead are now. Very little is said. There is not much said about hell either, but we do know that it has not "entered into the heart of man, the things which God hath prepared for them that love him."

By the same token, how do we know whether the picture of hell in the Bible is altogether literal or whether God tries to describe to the human mind something that is so terrible the human mind cannot comprehend it? And He has to use language that we can understand to describe something more terrible than we can imagine. I wonder sometimes if men and women in life could get a real glimpse of hell, if their minds would be the same after and if they could retain their sanity.

The Bible describes hell as a place where the worm dies not— that is, the soul of man—and where the fire is not quenched. That is a terrible picture. Eternal fire and eternal consciousness. But that, I believe, is a literal picture. If it is not a literal picture, it is an attempt by Almighty God to describe something that we could not comprehend, since there is no language in the words of man to make it clear.

Perhaps hell is nothing but vast and empty space set afire with the wrath of God, where the lost soul forever falls down, down, down, unsupported, crying, "Lost! Lost! Lost!" A lost sheep is pitiful. A lost dog can be pathetic. But what about a lost soul? There is no home awaiting him, no food from the hands of a kindly master. He is out in the vastness of a strange place with no one to care for him. A lost soul made of God for His presence, for the eternal joy of God's communion, for the eternal light of His home—but lost forever. You know, I do not know what hell will be like; but I do know this. If that is not a literal picture in the Bible, it is God's effort to describe something that is infinitely worse than there is language to describe.

I do not know what hell is like; but, thank God, no man has to know what hell is like if he is saved, for the redeemed are forever freed from hell. Our home is the eternal joy of God's presence. There will be a time when you will have to die, if the Lord tarries. You will go into His presence, or you will go into the place of His judgment forever. "We are not saved."

You know, you can be in doubt about many things in life, but no man can afford to be in doubt about his soul. Hell is too hot, and judgment is too sure, and eternity is too long to take a chance with your soul. I want to give you a twofold invitation tonight. I want to give you an opportunity to be saved. Remember, He came not to call the righteous but sinners to repentance. Is there anyone here who will say, "I am not saved, but I want to trust Christ as my Savior"?

I also want to ask you this: Who here will say, "Dr. Bob, when I think about eternity and hell and judgment and then think about God's grace and Christ's power to save, I feel guilty that I have not gone out to tell more people how to be saved. I want to dedicate my life afresh to witnessing for Christ, to try to snatch people from eternity, a lost eternity, and point them to Jesus. God helping me, I am going from this time forward to point men to Christ, to redeem the time, to do what I can to bring men to salvation.

Maybe you are not called to be a preacher. Maybe you are. Maybe somebody tonight has felt the call to preach. Maybe somebody feels the need to be a missionary; but I want to know how many of you, as a schoolteacher, as a housewife, as a merchant, as a farmer, are going to make the winning of souls the chief business of your life? Every Christian ought to give himself to this service.

If God has dealt with you about something in your life tonight, if you are lost and unsaved, if there are things in your life that dishonor God and need to be gotten rid of, I invite you to come now.

A Time When
Kings Go Forth to Battle
II Samuel 11:1

"And it came to pass, after the year was expired, at the time when kings go forth to battle, that David sent Joab, and his servants with him, and all Israel; and they destroyed the children of Ammon, and besieged Rabbah. But David tarried still at Jerusalem" (II Sam. 11:1).

This is the chapter that discusses David's failure and David's sin. If for no other reason, I would know this Book was not an ordinary Book because this chapter is included. When men write biographies, however sincere they try to be, they are either attracted to the subject of the biography or they dislike him intensely. As they write, they either play up his good qualities and omit some of the bad qualities, or they emphasize his weaknesses and failures and neglect to say the good things they ought to say about him. I suppose it is almost impossible to write an unbiased autobiography; but when God keeps the record, He keeps it clean, pure, and complete. David, the subject of this biography, was a man after God's own heart—a man who loved God and whom God loved, a man who except for one failure in his life was a man who greatly pleased God. This is the verse that introduces the chapter on his sin, but before we look at David's sin, let's say all the good things we can about him.

Let's go back and see the little boy, a young lad about twelve to fourteen years old. He was entrusted with the keeping of the sheep of his father. Watch him in the night as he looks up at the stars and says, "The heavens declare the glory of God; and the firmament sheweth his handywork." Listen to him as he takes his harp and tunes it and sings as he looks after his sheep. "The Lord is my shepherd; I shall not want." Watch him as, a little older, he goes out to destroy the wild beasts that come up to attack his sheep. He was brave, heroic, modest, poetic—all that you could expect a noble man in his youth to be.

See David when he is anointed to be king over Israel. The prophet comes, sent by God, to the house of Jesse, his father. He says to Jesse, "I want to see all your sons. Bring them in." The sons all come—fine, stalwart, manly men. As each one passes in front of him, God says, "That is not the one," until finally he has looked at all of them. He turns to Jesse and says, "Are these all your sons?"

Jesse turns to his wife and says, "Do we have any more?" She says, "Well, there is little David, but he is in the back pasture with the sheep." The prophet says, "Send for him." This young redhead comes in and God speaks to the prophet and says, "That is the man." The prophet anoints him to be the king of Israel in the place of Saul. He goes back to keeping his sheep. Some young men would have been so spoiled and flattered they would not have been fit to live with or of any use around the house after that, but this humble young man goes back to the everyday task. He is to be a king. The prophet has said so. The scent of the anointing oil is still upon his hair, but he goes back and keeps the sheep.

Look at him that time he goes up to check on his brothers at battle. There has been no news from the battlefront for a time. His parents become a little anxious about his brothers who are in the army, so they send him up with warm food cooked by their mother. I do not know exactly what that mother cooked. The Bible tells us of some things but not all, but if she had been an Alabama mother where I grew up, I know what she would have fixed. She would have made some biscuit—not the kind you cut out with a thimble but the kind you use a coffee can to cut out, a reasonable size, about six inches across, the kind you have to take two bites to eat. She fried some chickens. No frying-size chicken would have been safe around the house on an occasion like that. She made some nice homemade cakes and a few pies.

I used to visit an aunt of mine down in southeast Alabama. She was a real country lady. On Saturday she would cook enough to invite everybody from church to dinner with her on Sunday. She was a hospitable lady. She baked pies—apple pies, cherry pies, coconut pies, lemon pies, caramel pies—every good kind of pie you could think of—and then topped it off with a pecan pie. When people came to lunch, she would not say, "What kind of pie will you have?" She would say, "Will you have a piece of pie?" Then she would cut through the whole stack like a layer cake, and you got some of all of it.

I daresay this lady sent down to the spring and got the buttermilk that was there to be kept cool and gave him a big jug of buttermilk, and he went off to the camp. When he arrived, he found the soldiers were not busy about things the king's soldiers are usually occupied with. They were lining the front of the precipice, looking across to the Philistine army. There was a great giant of a man standing there. He was cursing God and defying the people of Israel, saying, "Send me out a champion. I will show you who is the god in this land. I defy you to send me out a champion." After a while, the army watching this drifted back to the work of polishing their armor and shining their boots and doing the things soldiers must do. Just then David ran into one of his brothers whom he had not been able to find before. David said, "Who is going to take that guy on?"

The brother replied, "What are you doing here? Why aren't you back with your sheep, little brother?"

"Never mind the sheep. They are being looked after. What about that giant that defies God and defies the armies of Israel? Who is going to take him on?"

"Look. You do not understand the psychology of cold war. If he can't get us worried, it is not going to hurt anything. He is just trying to get us panicky."

"Well, it seems like you are all scared enough already." Just then some others gather around and listen. Finally somebody tells the king about this argument. The brothers were inquiring about what David has in the basket, what he has brought from home, and what he is doing there; but he is not occupied with that now. He hands them the basket and says, "Let me go take that fellow on."

King Saul comes by. "What is this all about?"

"Listen. I have been able to kill lions and wild beasts. I will go take on that fellow. Isn't there anybody in this land that has any guts at all? I will go."

The king, who is a head taller than any man in the army, says, "Let's put my armor on you." I always wondered about this. Did he want credit for the victory, or did he really and sincerely want it to be done right? They put David in the king's armor, and he rattles around like one sardine in a tin can. He says, "Get me out of here. I cannot move, much less fight." He puts the armor aside and goes forth to the battle. He stops by the brook and picks up some round smooth stones and puts them in the purse at his side. He makes sure that his slingshot is untangled and ready to go, and then he goes out to meet the giant. The giant bends almost double with laughter at this little runt who has come out to fight him. David just lets go and whirls that thing around his head, and the stone goes; and the giant stops in the middle of laughter with a stone imbedded in his forehead. David goes up to him and draws this giant's own sword. It is so big it takes both hands for him to lift it. He cuts off the head of Goliath and goes back dragging the head behind him by the hair. He goes before Saul and rolls it like a bowling ball to the feet of the king.

What a man he was! He was a young boy, a champion, with the heart of a warrior and the soul of a giant. People began to shout, "Saul has slain his thousands but David his tens of thousands." The king's jealousy was aroused, and in his madness he later tried to slay this young man as David comforted him with a harp and the music to drive out the demons. David was forced to leave home. He went back to the wilderness and had to stay in the land of the Philistines for a while, but he never lifted his hand against the Lord's anointed, although he was delivered into his hands and David could have slain him. What a noble young man he was.

Well, David was a hero. Now he has conquered Jerusalem and made his capital there. Here he has established the government in this great city, and for the first time, he moves into his house, a new palace. There are walls of cedar that smell so fresh and springlike.

He looks out over the terrace and sees the city in the early light of dawn, gray as the mists rise and dark in the twilight time as the lights begin to twinkle. He is king now. He has had a hard career and a rough life. It is time for him to take a little rest. He tarries in Jerusalem. But wait, it is the time when kings go forth to battle. David sends Joab and the servants and a big army while he tarries in Jerusalem. It is the time when kings go forth to battle, but this king stays behind. It is the time when kings go forth to battle, but this king remains in the palace. It is the time when kings go out to battle, but this king takes his ease.

Young folks, you listen to me. The man who is not where he ought to be and the woman who is in the wrong place are in the place of sin and failure and of fall. I am talking to somebody here tonight who has tarried too long. You have held back yourself from God's will. The place of your dreaming is not the place of God's appointing. You are a rebel, and instead of exercising the strength of the position God has for you, you stay behind.

Oh, I am sure he found a good reason to stay there. Perhaps he said to himself, "Look, I have been in the battlefront for so many years now. I am all chafed from wearing the armor and carrying the helmet on my head. It is time I retired. They do not need me at the battlefront anymore." Or maybe he reasoned, "I need to get things settled here. This is a new capital. I am not sure about the government I have set up, but I'd better be sure that tax gatherers do not impose upon the people more than they should. I had better stay here to see that the law is enforced and the people are looked after and the water supply of the city is kept fresh. I am needed here to hear the cases that come before the judges. I need to be here." But it was the time when kings go forth to battle. Maybe he said to himself, "After all, Joab has been a faithful second lieutenant. I want to give him a chance now to prove himself. He is an old man. I am old, but let him have one great battle on his own so he can go down in history as a great conqueror. Let him go." But it was the time when kings go forth to battle.

David stays in Jerusalem. You had better make up your mind that you may fall into sin anywhere. I have seen it happen to men in the ministry. I have heard of it happening to evangelists in the midst of a great and successful evangelistic campaign. It can come at any time unless we walk in the fear of the Lord and in communion with Him, but let me tell you one thing. If you put yourself outside the will of God, you are already in sin and in the place where the Devil can trip you up and wreck your life. I have seen it happen over and over. David, taking his ease, rests in the afternoon. He wakes, rings the bell, and his servants come in and drape the royal robe over his shoulders. The folds fall so nicely to his ankles. They put on the gold sandals with the topaz clasps and bring in his great embellished girdle and give him cool sherbet to refresh himself and wake him up. He goes out to walk on the roof of the palace in the cool of the twilight and to look out over the city. He sees a woman bathing in the garden of the house near the palace, over the palace walls, a place where the trees are bare. There she is. Lust rises in his heart. He looks away. I am sure a good man looks away. You may sometimes have your sights drawn to things you ought not to see. You can look away. You may not be responsible for the first look, but you are to blame for the continuing look and the second look and the long look. He looks back, and he lusts for this woman. He sends for her and takes her. He gets her pregnant with a child, although he does not know that at the time.

Some weeks later he learns he is to be the father of her child. He is nervous now. He is in a bad fix, this man after God's own heart. This woman is the wife of a foreign officer, a Hittite, a man who came and swore allegiance to David because he admired and loved David. He has gone off to a battle the king should have been leading; but he has wronged a friend, wrecked a home, and now he resorts to deception and murder to cover his sin. Say, that is always the way sin goes. It starts off with a look and a lustful thought, a desire for something that is wrong, the taking, the consequences, the lies, the schemes, and the blood; but you cannot escape the consequences. You be sure your sin will find you out.

I had a letter just today. A man wrote me and said, "Dr. Bob, years ago I was a student in the Academy for just one year. I was a typical kid. I was taking drugs, drinking on the side, and smoking.

I lived in town. The University did not know all I was doing, but they knew I was not a good student and that I was a troublemaker. At the end of the year, I did not come back. I went somewhere else to college and continued my life of sin—only the sin got worse. My life was in a terrible mess until I faced up to my sin and got right with God. I am saved now. I believe if some student in Bob Jones University had been concerned about the sort of life I was living in the Academy, if somebody in the class with me and some of my friends had dealt with me about my sin and my hypocrisy and my pretense of religion, that I could have been straightened out and found the Lord in those days and escaped all the years that have gone between. Tell the students to deal with their friends about spiritual problems." It is interesting that letter came to my desk this morning, after I had been grieved and prayed, as I tried to sleep, about the students who last night would not speak to somebody still seated who needed to be dealt with and have a friendly hand laid on them. What a tragedy that is. Sin always gets worse and worse and worse, and there is no hope for sin except the grace of God. You cannot play with it. It will grow and devour you. You cannot put off the decision beyond the point of repentance. Death comes. Sad thing.

David writes a letter to Joab at the battlefront and says, "Take this Hittite and put him in the heat of the battle at the front line outside the city wall in the main attack, and then suddenly withdraw and leave him there exposed to the enemy." David does not sleep well for a few nights until he sees the messenger riding back, dusty and sweaty from a long ride. He comes into the palace and hands David the sealed parchment. David breaks it and reads, "It is all as you wanted. He was killed. He is dead." David throws the sheepskin parchment on the brazier that warms the room and thinks it is all settled. "Oh, that is all hidden now." In a few days when the mourning time is over, he takes the woman and marries her, and she bears a child. The sin is covered. Isn't that nice? Nobody knows. You can be sure people *did* know—the sneaky servants around the palace who listen behind closed doors, the maid of the woman he had wronged. Those things get about. You do not hide things you think somebody knows about. But somebody always knows. One day it will blossom into headlines.

David thinks it is all over, but sometime later an old prophet—not suited for the court, not smooth like the judges and the counselors, a rough man from the desert clothed in a skin—comes in and says, "I want justice, your Majesty."

"What kind of justice do you want?"

"There was a man who had a great flock of sheep, a rich man. He had a neighbor who had only one little pet lamb that he carried around like a pet dog. One day the rich man had a friend come in. He wanted to make a feast for him; but instead of using one of his own sheep, he went and took the man's little pet lamb and made a roast of it." David is furious, this man who is not concerned about a wronged woman and a bastard child and a servant that he betrayed, this man whose hands are dripping with blood, as it were. He is terribly concerned about a lost lamb. He rises up from the throne and says, "Tell me who that man is, and I will see that he pays."

An old broken fingernail is pointed in his face, and the old prophet says, "You are the man."

Conscience wakens. David thought it was dead and matters were forgotten. He had been resting in peace, but no more. Be sure your sin will find you out. David goes out of the room, rends his garment, puts on sackcloth and ashes, and in the darkness of his bedchamber calls out for forgiveness.

Praise God He can restore the joy of salvation. Isn't it strange that David had been without fellowship with God all those months and had not been aware of it? You can lose the Lord along the way of life somewhere because the Lord will not go the way *you* are going and will refuse to walk with you. It is hard to understand how people who have known the joy of the Lord and the strength of the Lord and the fellowship of the Lord, when these are suddenly gone, do not miss them. I can understand how sinners who have never known these things may not be aware of what this means, but once you have tasted and seen how good the Lord is and suddenly there is no longer the taste of the sweetness of honey in your mouth—that is a terrible thing.

God restores the joy, but, oh, the following consequences of the sin. A sister is raped by her brother. A brother is murdered by another brother because of the rape. There is rebellion in the family. There is a revolt against the king and almost the loss of his throne. There is a dead child, a broken heart. David, an old man in the room above the gate, watches for the return of Absalom, and hears he is dead, hanging by his hair in the trees—this wretched rebel of a son, unworthy of his father's love, for David did love him. David cries out brokenhearted, "O my son Absalom, my son, my son Absalom! would God I had died for thee, O Absalom, my son, my son!" Wretched son, seeking his father's throne and his father's life. It all followed the consequences of that sin. My friend, God can forgive your sin, but sometimes the consequences reach to the grave and beyond, and children bear the marks of the sins of the fathers unto the third and fourth generation of them that hate Him.

Well, I am glad the forgiveness is there, but I wish the sin had not been. If you are not hardhearted and if you were ever either a son or a father or a husband and you read this story, your heart will be touched, and you will be moved. Here is a wrecked home, a woman betrayed, her husband deceived, a friend murdered, hardheartedness, and fellowship with God broken. What a tragedy. It was the time when kings go forth to battle, but David tarried still in Jerusalem.

What Shall We Have Therefore?
Matthew 19:23-29

I am going to speak tonight from the same passage I used in the first revival meeting in the Rodeheaver Auditorium. It is an old sermon. I know I have not preached it here for some years, but somehow I feel led to preach it tonight.

A wonderful personality, Jesus Christ. How He drew people to Him—men, women, little children. Men came with the problems that confound men, women with the difficulties that women face, and the babies climbed out of their mother's laps and ran to Him. He said, "Let them come." No one ever came to God's Son with his problem unsettled or his need unmet.

On the occasion of our Scripture, our Lord had an interview with a rich young man, a fine, moral, upstanding young man. He came with an important question. He came about eternal life. "What good thing shall I do, that I may have eternal life?" He came to the right one. He came to the God of life, to the Giver of life, the one who breathed into man's nostrils the breath of life. But he thought he came to just a teacher, for he greeted Him with that Hebrew word which means teacher—good master. The Lord ignores the question for a moment to take issue with the salutation. He said, "Why callest thou me good? there is none good but one, that is, God." This is the implication: "Young man, you call me good, but you do not recognize my claim to be God. If I am not what I claim to be, I am not good."

My friend, if Jesus Christ is not more than a man, He is not a good man. The stupidest statement any of these so-called intellectuals can make is this: "I believe Jesus was a great teacher. I believe He was a great man. I believe He is a very noble character, but I do not believe He is God." If Jesus Christ is not God, He is a liar and a fraud and a crook! He claimed to be God. No good man would make a false claim. Over and over and over He took the name of deity for Himself. He said, "Before Abraham was I AM," and He used that unspeakable name of God. He sat on a well curb and talked to a woman about the Messiah. He said, "I that speak to thee am he." He said, "I and the Father are one." "He that hath seen me hath seen the Father." Anybody who tries to tell you that Jesus made no claims to be God is a fool. It is obvious that He is God. He claimed to be God, and only God has the answer to eternal life.

Having asserted His right to answer the young man's question, He said to him, "You want to know how to have eternal life? Go and sell what you have and give to the poor." But first He said, "Keep the commandments." Does this strike you as strange that the Lord should say, "Keep the commandments"? Does not the Book say that we are saved by grace through faith, not of works, lest any man should boast? Yes, it does, but what is sin? Sin is the transgression of the law. What is the law? The law is the Word of God as given for man to obey. If you have never sinned, never violated God's law in thought or word or deed, you do not need to be saved. If you have kept God's law perfectly with mind and heart and soul, you have no need for a Savior. He came not to call the righteous, but sinners to repentance. If you have never sinned, you have never lost your fellowship with God.

But the trouble is that every man has sinned and "none is righteous, no, not one." It is wonderful how this condemnation is passed on all men so that "all have sinned and come short of the glory of God." Therefore, I have not kept the commandments. I cannot keep the commandments, and he that is guilty in one violates them all. The standards of the Lord are high. He that looks to lust is an adulterer. What does that mean? It means a man who looks with lustful gaze at a woman and says, "I would take her if I could," is, in God's sight, as guilty as if he had taken her. "He that hates his brother is a murderer." Hate is the root of murder, and any man who hates and despises another man could, if he lets hate have free range, kill that man. There are lots of murderers that never shed any blood. It makes them sick to see blood, so they do not kill. They are afraid they will have to go to jail. They do not kill somebody because they could not get by with it; but if a man hates somebody enough he would kill him, in God's sight he is guilty of murder. It is out of the heart that the issues of life come.

"Keep the commandments." "Which one?" It is strange that he would ask that question. He must have known the Decalogue forwards and backwards. I think he did, but he expected some new commandment from this new rabbi; but he does not get a new one. He gets just part of the old ten. The Lord only gives him six of the ten. That is significant. Wherever a thing like this appears in the Bible, always look into it and ask yourself why. Why does the Lord give this man six commandments? Which does He leave out? "Thou shalt have no other gods before me. Make not graven images. Take not the name of the Lord thy God in vain, and keep holy the sabbath day." He does not mention those at all. He mentions the others: "Thou shalt not kill. Thou shalt not steal. Thou shalt not commit adultery. Thou shalt not covet." That is stated there as "Thou shalt love thy neighbor as thyself."

He gave him not ten but six commandments. The reason for that is He is dealing with a self-righteous, moral young man. The six commandments He gives are the six commandments that govern men in their relationship to other men. He does not say anything about the four commandments that govern us in relationship to God—no graven images, not taking the Lord's name in vain, no other gods before Him. He does not give him those because He is dealing with the kind of young man who says, "I treat everyone as I want everybody else to treat me." This young man is so holy that he is just kind of waiting for a vacancy in the Trinity to apply for it—that kind of fellow who is so self-satisfied that he is proud of his righteousness. He is one of these fellows who says, "I am not so bad." The Lord gave him the six commandments, and what did he say? He said, "All these things have I kept from my youth up."

I think he thought he told the truth. I do not believe he knew he was a liar. I honestly believe that he was sincere, that he had gotten his gold honorably, that he was not an adulterer. He was as nice as anybody here in this place tonight. But, you see, it is what a man is that sends him to hell, not what he does. You go to hell not for what you do. No man ever went to hell because he killed a man. No man ever went to hell because he stole. A man goes to hell not because of what he does but because of what he is. Do you know how you can tell what you are? What is the thing you would instinctively do if you could get by with it and nobody would ever know? That is the way you judge yourself. A man who gives, not letting his right hand know what his left hand does or vice versa, is a charitable, godly man. He does not do it to be rewarded. He does it because he loves and loves to give. If you would kill, then you are in your heart a murderer; and men go to hell for what they are. What you do, you do because of what you are. A fish swims, a bird flies—just because he is a fish or a bird. A man walks upright because he is a man. Some animals walk on four legs. Some of the primates walk on their hind legs but use the knuckles of the forearms to support themselves. But man walks upright because he is a man. What you do you do because of what you are; and if you are a sinner, you are going to sin inevitably because the thoughts of the human heart are wicked thoughts. The natural man cannot do works of righteousness because he is dead unto righteousness. It is as simple as that.

"What lack I yet?" asked the young man. Thank God, there was some hope for him. He knew that was not enough. Then the Lord said, "Go and sell that thou hast, and give to the poor, and thou shalt have treasure in heaven: and come and follow me." Give to the poor and have treasure in heaven? No. I can give my body to be burned and find no profit in it. It is the second part of the command that brings salvation—"Come and follow me." Why then does the Lord tell this young man to sell everything he had and give it to the poor? Because he knew he was hindered from following Him because of his wealth and responsibilities. It is never right, as you have heard so many times from this platform, to do wrong in order to get a chance to do right. For this man to walk away and leave his business in a mess would have been wrong. God had entrusted him with the responsibilities of wealth. Now the Lord said, "Go and discharge those responsibilities, sell all you have, give it away, cut the ties that bind you, raise the anchor so you can follow me." But the Bible tells us that the young man went away with sorrow for he had great possessions.

Poor rich young man! He is one of the saddest characters in all the Bible to me. We do not know his name. He was just a young man who came and asked and went away. We might have learned his name if he had followed Jesus. It would have been written in the Lamb's book of life, but instead he went back to write it again on the tax rolls of Jerusalem. Did you ever stop to think that I might have read the Scripture tonight from the pen of this young man? If he had followed the Lord, he might have been used as some of the rest were to give us a gospel in the Word of God. But instead he went back to balance his bank book in Jerusalem. This young man might have become a companion of the apostles and a fellow of the disciples, but instead he went back to mingle with the merchants and brokers in Jerusalem. He might have become the heir of a mansion in glory, but instead he went back to his palace in Jerusalem, a lovely place no doubt, with marble floors and tapestry-covered walls and perfumed oil burning in golden lamps. He went back to lush wines and heavy banquets and silken robes in the wardrobe. Maybe he had a summer villa on the slopes of the Mount of Olives, and he went there to stand between the marble columns to look out over his estate. His grain was like a golden sea rippling in the meadow. His olive orchards were like green carpets on the hillside. He chose the things he could touch and see and taste and handle and enjoy, and he lost eternal life.

Poor rich young man! "What shall it profit a man, if he shall gain the whole world, and lose his own soul? Or what shall a man give in exchange for his soul?" Young folks, what do you value your soul as being worth? God values it as more than all the universe, but some men sell their souls for a cheap thrill, for a love of sin, for the approval of the ungodly, and for the smile of the enemies of the Almighty. But God says your soul is worth more than the universe. And this young man held his so lightly. He weighed it in the scale of gold and silver and lands and houses, and he lost eternal life. Do you wonder I call him a poor young man? I am sure that the Lord's heart was heavy. He desires not the death of any. I do not think anything grieves God more than the waste of potentialities of life. God sees what you could be by His grace and what you will not be because of self-will and sin. I think it breaks God's heart.

That is the moment that Peter chose to ask the question that is our text tonight. Do not worry. I am almost half through. I am just putting the text where it belongs for a change—in the middle of a sermon. It is a good idea to preach to the text before you depart from it, so I am just being guilty of good homiletics tonight and putting the text in the middle.

This is the text: "Lord, we did it. What are we going to get out of it?" I grant you it did not sound like that when I read it in the King James Version. That sounds like "Hard News for Sinful Man." I love this King James Version. Cadent syllables march by like armies with plumes in their helmets and banners afloat. It sounds like the throbbing of a great organ. It sounds almost respectable in the King James Version, "Behold, we have forsaken all, and followed thee; what shall we have therefore?" It sounds almost decent and nice; but in the blunt Aramaic that Peter used, it was just as rough as this in modern "slanguage." "What is the payoff for loving you, Lord? What are we going to get out of this thing?" It is the question of the hireling and the servant, not the question of a friend. I wince for Peter every time I read it. It is just like him. He had a gift for saying the wrong thing at the wrong time. He was a married man. At least, he had a mother-in-law, and no man ever had a mother-in-law without benefit of a wife. I have often wished she could have gone along to keep him straight—I mean, the wife, not the mother-in-law. You married men know how effective a wife is when you start to say the wrong thing. Before you can open your mouth, she kicks you under the table. I wish some doctor could explain to me the connection between a man's shin bone and his jawbone. She works one, and you work the other. But if Peter's wife had gone along, he would have been too crippled to walk. He would have had no skin on his shins at all. He always said the wrong thing.

Nothing Peter ever said was worse than this: "What are we going to get for loving You?" The Lord could have answered him in so many ways. He could have said, "Peter, what have you left?" I can see that redhead scratching his hair until the old fish scales flew. "Let me see, Lord. I left my house." He had—a fisherman's house with walls of driftwood plastered with mud and thatched with straw, with pebbles for the floor and a rickety table and a stool or two. Not much of a house, but it was home. You do not have to have crystal chandeliers blazing from walls like bouquets of diamonds. A mother's smile can make a mountain cabin radiant. The footprint of a little child in a sandy floor is lovelier than an Oriental rug. The Lord said, "Follow me," and Peter opened the door on the squeaky hinges and went off after Jesus. He must have often remembered that house on the beach because God's Son had no place to lay His head. He used to go up into the hills to spend the night. Up there were no walls of driftwood—just the cold wind that poured down from northern peaks. Up there was no canopy of straw—just the stars looking down through the holes in the sky that the rain came through. He did not even have a pallet of straw. His bed was the shale of a hillside, and he had a rock for a pillow. But in the wilderness his bedfellow was the Son of God. I say he made a good bargain when he left his house. You had better dwell alone in the desert with God's Son than to live in a king's palace without Him.

"What else did you leave, Peter?" "Well, Lord, I left my nets." Fishing nets—nothing wrong with fishing. I like to fish. That is not quite the truth. I like to catch fish. It is not the same thing. I know some people who go fishing all day and come back with nothing and say they liked it. I think they are lying. Whether I am preaching or whether I am fishing, I like to catch something. There is nothing wrong with fishing unless fishing gets in the way of something important, but God wanted Peter to catch men. He would not have been any use to Jesus with that fishnet on his back. He would have been caught and trapped and tripped and tied in his own twine if he had tried to follow the Lord with those nets on his back. I am glad he left them. Maybe that is why some of you have not had any more success in your Christian life. You brought too many nets along— nets of old friendships and old pleasures and old ambitions and old dreams. The Lord expects you to leave the nets.

One night up above Galilee there was a hungry crowd. I think there must have been about thirty thousand people. The Bible says there were five thousand men besides the women and children, and if men went to church in those days in the same proportion they go in our day, there were about five women and kids for every man in the crowd. That makes thirty thousand. That was a sorry crowd. The babies were all crying. It was supper time, and Mama had left the bottle and the pablum at home. The men all had tired feet and empty stomachs. If there is anything meaner than a hungry man, it is a hungry man in tight shoes. The women were all cross-eyed from trying to keep one eye on the husband and the other eye on the kids all day.

But the Lord solved that problem. He can solve every problem. There was a little boy who had his lunch. That is the greatest miracle in Scripture. Did you ever know a kid about twelve years old who forgot to eat at twelve o'clock? Here it is sundown, and the kid has been so interested in the Lord that he forgot to eat! I do not know another miracle like that in the Bible. What a tribute to the power of our Lord! This little boy pulls the coattail of an apostle as he goes by and says, "Will you give the Lord my lunch?" He did not give it to the crowd. Do you waste your life in social service? Give yourself to the Lord. He will bless and break you, and you will go farther. It was not much—a few loaves and a few fish, but it was all the Lord needed. God does not want any more than all you have, and He will not settle for less. Get that straight. Nothing is too big for Jesus, and no gift is too small if it is all you have.

The Lord took it; He blessed it; He broke it; and Peter had a share in the miracle. He waited on tables that night. When I was a student, a freshman in Bob Jones College, I used to wait on tables. The waiters always ate after everybody else got through, and there were two things wrong with that job. I was so clumsy I broke so many dishes that I owed the school money at the end of the month; and whenever we had what I liked to eat, everybody else liked it too, and it was all gone before we got a chance at it. Here there were twelve basketsful left over and no dishes to break. The AFL, CIO, and Waiters' Union could not do better for you than that. Peter took some of the broken bread and broken fish and passed it out. "Grandpa, would you like a piece of fish? It is all right; you do not need teeth. The Lord blessed it. Just gum it, grandpa." "Lady, wouldn't you like to give the baby a biscuit?" By and by peace and quiet settled on the hillside. You talk about the thrill of catching fish, of pulling in a laden net all aflutter with silvern denizens of the deep. That is no thrill to compare with the miracle of broken fish that feeds thousands. I say that if it is for the thrill of that moment that Peter left his nets, he made a good bargain.

"What else did you leave, Peter?" "Lord, I left Nancy Belle." It may not have been Nancy Belle. I expect it was a nice Jewish name like Rachel or Ruth or Elizabeth or Rebecca—but he must have had a name for his boat. Fishermen always name their boats. As a boy he had gone up into the hills, and he and his brothers had cut the trees and dragged them down to the beach. They had laid the keel and fixed the planks and caulked the seams and set the mast. Night after night he had fished from her decks in the moonlight. The sails were like wings overhead, and she responded like a live thing to his touch on the rudder. It must have grieved him most to leave his boat, but he left it—keel up on the beach, gaping open at the seams. The Lord said, "Follow me," and the boat was left.

But another time he and the disciples were in another boat, and the Lord came walking on the water. Peter saw Him, and he said, "Lord, if that be Thou, bid me come." The Lord said, "Come." Peter jumped out of that boat. I remember thirty years ago I said that up in Boston; and after the service, a typical New England dowager came up. You can always tell those rich, Back Bay women because their old black hats have been handed down for so many generations they have turned brown. That is the mark of a rich Back Bay Bostonian—an old black brown hat. She came up and looked at me through her lorgnette. I did not know anybody still wore their glasses on a fork handle. She looked at me through those things and said, "Dr. Jones, you said that Peter jumped. Did it use that word in the gospel?"

Between you and me, I was not going to tell her, while she was looking at me through those eyeglasses, that I did not know just what the word was. So I said, "You mean you have never read it?" You cannot imagine Peter doing anything but jumping. He always moved first and thought about it later. Can you imagine Peter taking off his shoe for fear it would get wet and putting a foot over the side and trying the wave to see if it was solid? I said, "Besides, lady, it is only the man who jumps when Christ says, 'Come,' that has the faith to walk on water." Talk about travel—airplanes, ocean liners—I would rather travel that walk than any way man ever invented. There is a great big wave, and Peter says, "I have to climb that one." He gets to the top and is out of breath. While he waits to rest, he kind of kicks the foam around like pebbles, and then he just slides down the other side.

But he went down. The Scripture says that he saw the waves were contrary. I know what happened. He took his eyes off the Lord. Faith gave way to self-confidence. He looked around to see if the boys in the boat were getting an eyeful of his performance. He looked around to say, "John, old boy, how am I doing? James, come on. Let us see you try this," and down he went. The water almost closed over him, and he cried, "Save me, Lord, I perish!" A hand went out. Thank God a hand always goes out when that cry goes up from a sinking soul. And Peter was pulled from the gaping deep, and there was an arm around his waist. That is the hand that holds all the oceans in its hollow. That is the arm that sustains the universe. That is the right arm of His righteousness. You talk about boats and sailing. My friend, it is no thrill to compare with the thrill of God's presence and sustaining arms in the midst of a stormy sea. I say that if it were for that moment that Peter left his nets, he made a good bargain.

The Lord did not ask him to name what he had left. He could have answered him in such a way as to break Peter's heart. He could have said, "Yes, Peter, you have left all. Did you ever stop to think what I left? I left anthems in heaven and songs of morning stars. Up there they cried, 'Holy, holy, holy,' but I left those hosannas to come down and hear men curse me and say, 'Crucify him.' I had a garment of light and a robe of glory, but I laid them aside to put on a mantle of flesh for you, Peter. I left a throne for a cross and a crown for thorns. Peter, I left something too." I think if the Lord had answered Peter like that, he would have done what he did another night when he had denied Him. He would have gone out to weep bitterly. No, the Lord said, "No man ever leaves anything for My sake but he receives a hundredfold and has everlasting life."

Does it pay to be a Christian? My friend, it is the only life that does pay. If there were no hereafter and no hell to shun and heaven to gain, if there were nothing but this life, do not wake me up. If it is nothing but a dream, it is a wonderful dream. But it is not a dream. Beyond this life is eternity, and when you weigh everything in the light of eternity, you will realize how much it pays to follow Jesus. Peter's problem was that he was on the other side of the cross. He had not yet seen the Lord die. He had not had that marvelous experience in the upper room.

Let us see Peter a few months later. After the death and the resurrection, he and another disciple go up to the house of prayer, to the temple; and there is a beggar who sits at the gate—a poor, twisted, deformed man. He holds out a crippled arm and says to Peter, "Will you give me some money?" Peter said (remember, this is the one who said, "What will I get?" but now has been transformed by a vision), "Silver and gold have I none; but such as I have give I thee: In the name of Jesus Christ of Nazareth rise up and walk." A lame man leaped into the temple praising God that day because Peter had left all to follow. It is only the man or woman who leaves all to follow Christ who knows the joy of God's power worked out through his life to bless needy men.

Peter told the truth. He had left all. Have you? Who here bears about in his body any marks for the Lord Jesus? Who has known the sting of the lash, the burn of the fire, the bite of the sword? Who has had to go to distant lands for Christ's sake? You say, "Wait, Dr. Bob, I have not had to leave my family. They are Christians too. I am not called to be a missionary." Well, tell me, do you love the Lord enough to go if you are called, and do you love Him more than you love any earthly tie—more than that boy or that girl? God who judges sin by the attitude of the heart judges surrender the same way. He may never ask you to die, but there is a crown laid up for those who are faithful up to death. We call it the martyr's crown.

You do not have to be a martyr to get that crown. It is really the crown of faithfulness—faithful up to the very point of death and through death if necessary—and the Lord rewards you as if you had died. He may never call you to leave your loved ones and go to some distant place; but if you love Him enough to go, more than anything else, He will reward you as if you had gone. Peter told the truth.

Students in Bob Jones University, visitors, friends, when you look at yourself, what do you see in yourself to the glory of the Lord Jesus? I am going to tell you a story now, and I am through. Years ago in Bob Jones College, when the school was small, a freshman girl came into my office. She put down her violin. She had been to a music lesson. She said, "Dr. Bob, I want to talk to you. I do not have the joy a Christian ought to have. Can you help me find the trouble?"

I was surprised. I remembered the letter I had had from that girl the previous summer. She had said, "Dear Dr. Jones: I was just saved last week in a meeting in my home church conducted by one of the preacher boys from Bob Jones. I have been playing my violin in a dance combo, but now I want to play it for the Lord. I want to come to Bob Jones College because I know you have a good music department; but more than that, I want to be with Christian students and a godly faculty. My family is opposed to my coming. They are unsaved. They say I can go to a teachers' college here in my own state of North Carolina, but I believe the Lord wants me there. I believe God will help supply my needs." She made application. The day she came to see me, she had been here about three months.

I said, "Dorothy, is there any sin in your life?"

She said, "No, Dr. Bob, not if I know my heart."

I said, "Are you holding anything back from God?"

She said, "No. I had to leave my family. I have not even had a letter from my parents since I came here three months ago."

I opened the violin case and took out the fiddle. I said, "How about this?"

She said, "Don't you remember that I told you I was just going to play that for the Lord from now on?"

I put the violin back and closed the case. I said, "Wait a minute, Dorothy. This is God's violin. You are going to play it. Suppose God told you to keep your 'cotton-picking hands' off His fiddle. How about that?"

She said, "You don't think God wants me to give up my music?"

"No, I don't think so. I think God gave you talent to be used and invested, but He may know that, like Isaac, this is the thing you love most; and He may ask you to lay it on an altar untouched. How about it?"

She began to cry. She said, "I just love music too much to give it up. I will play the violin for the Lord, but I just could not live without music."

I said, "Dorothy, I think we have found your trouble." I watched her the next day at chapel. In those days we had about five hundred students. It was easy to spot her. Everybody was singing, smiling like a noonday sky in summer; but there was one cloud. It was Dorothy's face. I prayed for her in my heart all through that chapel and the next day and the next. Then the next day I could not find her while they sang. She had her mouth open so wide I could not see her face for her mouth. But after we got through singing, she was still smiling all the way across her face. I thought, "She has settled it." She came in to see me later that day and put the fiddle on my desk. She said, "Dr. Bob, I want you to see God's fiddle. If He wants me to play it, I will play it for His glory; but if He says, 'Dorothy, never play another note,' that is all right too. I love Him more than I love music or anything."

That is what it means to forsake all to follow. It means to have no friends except the friends of His choosing, no desire except the desire to please Him, no joy except the joy of His smile, and no will except the will to do His will. "He that doeth the will of God abideth forever."

His Love to Us Is Wonderful
II Samuel 1:19-27

Will you open your Bibles, please, to II Samuel 1, beginning to read at verse 19. This is surely the loveliest eulogy ever written over dead men—one deserving and the other not. It is amazing how noble a man David was. He owed nothing to Saul. Saul had abused him, broken treaties with him, sought his life, attempted to kill him personally, pursued him into the wilderness, tried to break up his family. He did everything he could to ruin and destroy David. Now hearing that he is dead, David forgets the wickedness of Saul's latter years and the meanness personally extended him by the king. His thoughts go back to the early years when Saul, taller by a head than any other man in Israel, first came to be king. He remembered his victories, the trophies he brought back, and the wealth he poured out upon the kingdom. He remembered all the good things he could. He tried in this eulogy to forget his evil, his betrayal of God's trust when He sent him into a land to slay all the people and bring nothing back. Saul had disregarded that and brought back a king in chains and the best of the cattle for his own herd. David remembers only the good things about him. What a lovely tribute he pays him here.

I think this eulogy was written primarily for Jonathan. What a friend Jonathan was to David. Their friendship has become classic. They were two noble and masculine men who became strong friends—the older man Jonathan and the younger man David. Jonathan, who could have been king, stepped aside and helped his friend David, against his father's wishes, to be prepared to receive the crown. A wonderful friendship. Happy is the man who has friends like this. I think it is because of his friendship for Jonathan that David wrote this song. Lovely words—"Thy love to me is wonderful." Thank God for good friends and what they mean to us here and hereafter.

I am going to do something I tell the preacher boys not to do. I am going to take a text out of a context (that generally makes it but a pretext for a sermon) because I want to deal with something that is so beautifully touched upon in the Word of God, and this very simple text somehow sums it all up for us. Let's take this tribute to Jonathan from his friend David and give it to the one who is the friend of sinners, the root and offspring of David. Let's say of the Lord Jesus Christ, "His love to us is wonderful"—so wonderful there was never any love like it, so wonderful it passes our understanding and goes far beyond our comprehension. It has to be experienced but can never be fully experienced until we stand in His presence and behold the wounds in His body.

His love to us is wonderful. It is wonderful in the first place because He gave Himself for us. He loves us, and there is nothing in us lovely. That is a terrible thing to say to a modern congregation. God looking at you, the best of you, does not see anything there deserving of His love. Suppose everybody in this place could see you tonight just like God sees you. Suppose I could take aside the veil that covers your past and we could see all you have done in all your life. Do you think you would be respected in this company?

Let's go deeper still. Let's burrow deep down into your hearts and see the blackness of some thoughts that are there—the intents and purposes, the thing you would have done if you could have done it. The dreams you dreamed when you had nothing else to think upon. The secrets and thoughts and intents of the heart are open to Him, and He loves us still. A friend I have known for some years, a talented, gifted woman, went into eternity a few days ago. She was a woman who loved good music, who loved art, who appreciated Bob Jones University for the good things that are here, who listened on the radio to our programs as they go out, but who died without Christ and is tonight in hell. She could not see herself as a sinner. She said, "I do not like to hear you talk about sin, about Jesus' having died for sin. How could a good God send anyone to hell?" Poor woman. Her trouble was that she never could see God as He is revealed in the Word of God because she never could see sin as God sees sin.

The thing you regard as light and unimportant, God sees for what it is—rebellion against Him, wicked thoughts, evil imaginings. There are many things that pass today in society as strange and sometimes laughable phenomena which are really sin. This Women's Lib Movement is a monument to sin. It was founded because women are not able and willing to accept the place God has given them. They want to be more than what God intended them to be or (to put it kindly) different from what God made them to be. That is rebellion. That is sin. Man's attitudes today are in rebellion against God's ordinance for man's good. Imagine. Man is rebelling against the King of heaven and saying, "I will not. I will not be what you want me to be. I will take a place to which I am not appointed. I will rise up and shake my puny, little, skinny fingers in your face and say, 'I won't,' to Almighty God."

It is strange how much folly there is today. Sin. It is a terrible thing, and it can lead to the most awful crimes. Maybe you sit here and say, "I am not a murderer. I never killed anybody." Well, tell me, was there ever a person you so disliked that you could not stand the sight of him? Did you ever as a child say about somebody, "I wish he was dead"? Did you? You are a murderer. God says you do not have to kill; but if you hate a brother in your heart, you are a murderer because hatred is the seed of murder. Many a man has not murdered only because he does not like the sight of blood. He fears the consequences of the act, or he cannot find a time, place, and method to do what he would like to do. He who looks on a woman to lust after her is already an adulterer in his heart. The Bible says, "Keep thy heart with all diligence; for out of it are the issues of life." What you do you do first in your heart. It begins there as an imagination. "I would like to do this. If I could, I would." God sees that heart; and if you let that heart go uncontrolled and untamed, unmodified by law and society and the teaching of the gospel that has gone over the world, if you let yourself go, you could be the worst lecher and the bloodiest murderer the world has ever known. We cannot understand how a man can go from one woman to another, killing them, hiding their bodies in the hill somewhere, trying to pile up a number of victims.

There are many things we cannot understand. My friend, when sin has its way and fulfills its course, these are the results. There never was a generation in which sin has been so lightly regarded as this generation. Murder. Millions of babies killed in the womb. My friend, those mothers who murder those children are just as guilty as that woman who pushed the car with her two little boys into the lake near here. The child in the womb is a being with an immortal soul. God has given life and immortality to that child. The mother takes the life. Well, thank God, in the innocence of that unborn child there is hope of immortality. That child will stand someday in heaven, fully grown no doubt, and point his finger at the mother and say, "You killed me." My friend, there is going to be much grief in eternity because men are what they are. If you could recognize sin as it must look to a holy God, a God so holy He cannot tolerate sin, who sees every evil as the evil that it is, then you would understand why there must be a hell and why men go there.

But it is not God's will that men go to hell. Men go to hell in a final act of rebellion against the will of God. The Lord is "not willing that any should perish, but that all should come to repentance." Men go to hell because they will not go to heaven. The Lord has made a way to make it possible. The Lord sent someone to preach the gospel so you will find the way. The Lord has given you His precious Word so that you may find revealed in this Word God's love for you, how He wants you in heaven. Finally, you won't go there; and God says, "All right. Depart from me ye workers of iniquity." That includes every person who has had evil thoughts or who has idly gossiped or lied or robbed, who has failed as a father because he did not let God into his heart, who has been an evil mother because she pushed her daughters into society and drove them into lives of sin because she was ambitious. God sees every sin, and God will finally say to the sinner, "Go away." God does not say it with joy. God says it with grief.

Don't you think a Savior who loved men enough to die to get them to heaven must be heartbroken when He sees that He has seemingly failed with some and they won't come to heaven because they will not put their faith and trust in Him? If there is anybody you can afford to trust, it is Jesus Christ. He never betrayed any man who put his faith in Him. He never lied to anybody. He gives us the breath of air we breathe and an opportunity to live with Him forever. He offers Himself as the sacrifice for our sin. Seeing that sin as horrible as it is, He took it upon Himself. Imagine the immaculate Son of God willing to be made sin for you. He took your sin that you might have His life. Sin cannot go unpunished. God is not a venal judge who overlooks guilt. God declares that the soul that sinneth shall die. If it did not die and go to hell forever, the rebellious, the unconverted, the unregenerate would destroy heaven if they got there, as they well nigh have destroyed this world and eventually will. The wages of sin is death to nations. It is death to men. It is death to women. It is death to all who love sin and cling to it. Jesus Christ, seeing us as sinners, loves us still. The only way we can love the unlovable is by God's grace. One of the surest signs that a man knows Christ is that he will go out of his way to pick up somebody that is lost in sin and unattractive and try to bring that one to Christ through care and tender teaching.

His love is wonderful in the second place because there is nothing in us that is loving toward God. We love everything about ourselves. We love our desires. We love our comforts. We love our money. We love our happiness. Man's great sin is love of self. Oh, there are lots of idols. The pagans used to make them, but you do not have to make idols. You just stumble upon them. The greatest idol in most lives is "self." You love yourself, but you do not love God. No man comes to love God except as the Holy Spirit of God comes into his heart and touches that heart with His tender compassion and brings him to love God. No man of himself loves God. We love iniquity rather than righteousness.

Man left to himself untaught and unrestrained will go into everything evil, but how few people love that which is good. One of the great sins of our day is the love of rock music. Rock music is evil and vile and destructive. Do not think people are just being extreme when they take a stand against that. It appeals to the flesh.

71

I read today a report of a rock concert and the people who put on that rock concert—"Christian" rock. They say, "The difference between our music and the music of the world is this: our music has sacred words." Further in the report they admitted that half the time you could not hear the words for the noise. My friend, it appeals to the flesh and to the flesh alone. The words are sordid and not honoring to God. They are cheap words and not scriptural language, but men love them because the human heart turns to iniquity as sparks fly upward in the fire. You do not love God. If you loved God, you would honor Him all your life. If you loved God, you would be glad to suffer for Him. You would be glad to be identified with Him. When a man loves a woman, he cannot say too much about her. He does not want to talk about anything else except that girl. In his opinion she is perfect. She may be as ugly as sin itself, but in his eyes, she is a beauty.

My friend, Jesus Christ, who is the Rose of Sharon and the Lily of the Valley, who is as lovely as a spring morning and as beautiful as a starry night, loves us. But we fled from Him. We refused Him. We hid from Him and despised Him, but He loved us. "Herein is love, not that we loved God, but that he loved us, and sent his Son to be the propitiation for our sins." It is only His immaculate, wonderful love that can bring men to love Him. Oh, He is worth all the adoration and all the praise and all the glory and all the service and all the hallelujahs and all the hosannas. Every drop of blood in our veins ought to beat for Him, and every glance ought to be in His direction. Every word ought to be spoken to tell of His goodness and His grace and His love.

He loved us. While we were His enemies, Christ died for us. Perhaps for a good man some will even dare to die, but evil as we are, He died for us. We are the opposite of all He is and all He loves and all He wants, as a pure and perfect Deity. Yet He loves us. He loves us more than angels. He loves us more than the stars He made, and He made them because He loves beauty. He put them there as lights in the darkness to remind us of the one who put them there. Someday He is going to push them all aside and take them out of the way. There is going to be a new earth and a new heaven. There will be no stars or sun, for the Lord God is the light. Those who turn many to righteousness will shine like the stars forever. He loves us more than anything He ever made. He loves every poor sinner, every victim of drugs and drink and tobacco, those who are lustful and wicked and dishonest and crooked and profane. He not only loves them but died for them. He loves them with an everlasting love even as they go to hell in rejection. His love is wonderful.

Finally, it is wonderful in its expression. The fact that Jesus Christ died for us is the final expression of love. What more can man do for his country than to die for it? What more can a man do for his family than to give his life for them? What more could Jesus Christ do to demonstrate His love than to die for us? All things were made by Him and for Him, and for His honor and glory they were created. He left all the glory to come down to all the squalor of earth. He left all the angelic music to come to hear the shouts of war and battle on the ground. He left the hallelujahs to come down here to hear men cry, "Crucify Him! Away with Him!" He expressed that love in the finest way that love can be expressed.

David and Jonathan first met when David comes back with the head of Goliath. He rolls it like a bowling ball before the feet of the king. Saul looks up and sees David; but Jonathan, who is standing by his father the king, sees David also. Those two noble men—the elder and the younger—become the closest of friends. Jonathan takes David into the royal tent and says to him, "That old shepherd's cloak you are wearing is not good enough for you. Let me give you a prince's robe." He gave him a prince's robe, a tunic all purple and gold embroidered. He gave him his girdle—soft kid's skin, perhaps with a topaz clasp. He gave him his sandals, his bow, his arrow. David stands under the king's banner in the king's tent, and he looks like the son of a king. Then Jonathan says, "Do you need anything else? What else do you want? I will give it to you."

That is what the Lord Jesus does for us. He gives us all good things. We are shod with the preparation of His gospel. He gives us His robe of righteousness to wear. He gives us the sword of His Spirit, the Word of God. We come into the royal pavilion. The King's banners are flying from the top post. He says, "Do you want anything else? You ask for it." Listen to this wonderful verse: "He that spared not His own Son, but freely delivered Him up for us all, how dare He, having given Him, hold back anything?" It is not that way in the Authorized Version, but that is the full meaning of it. "How shall he not with him also freely give us all things?" "No good thing will he withhold from them that walk uprightly." If He gives you His Sonship with the Father, if you are accepted in the beloved by the Father, if you become an heir of a mansion in glory and a house on high and eternal life and joy forever, do you think He would hold back anything else? Oh, His love is wonderful. My friend, love demands love. Love suffers without love. When your heart goes out to somebody, you want some affection from them.

Are you a Christian? Have you taken the gift of salvation? Are you washed in that blood? Is your faith fixed in Jesus Christ? Do you have a home in heaven? Do you have all His promises to be with you and never to leave you nor forsake you? What have you given to Him? What about the odd moments, the ragged actions, the things that do not seem so important to you and that are not necessary for your happiness and for your joy? Do you know how you can tell whether you love the Lord or not? Do you love Him enough to have nothing if that is His wish for you? Now, honestly, are you willing to be poor for His sake? Are you willing to have every man hate you, have the people you admire turn against you, to go hungry if need be, to lay down your life for Him? My friend, that is the kind of love He gave to us, imperfect as we are and false and full of sin.

Do not talk about being dedicated until everything is on the altar, until your highest joy is the joy of pleasing Him, your most precious treasure the salvation you have, the diamond of your heart the love of Jesus. We cannot give men life by dying, but the Lord wants all we have. If it is necessary to die for His glory, He wants that. Salvation is free. He demands nothing for that, but my, how He craves our love. Angels quickly obey Him, but sometimes we turn back. We want what we want; but, my friend, if you love the Lord Jesus, you will want Him to have everything you have. You will recognize that having given Him all, you are still an unprofitable servant—a servant who is not always faithful, who is not alert, who is not quick to go, who balks and holds back and tries to dicker. The only true servant is one who loves the Master enough to do what the Master wants and tries to please the Master. He is the greatest of all masters and the tenderest of all bosses. He wants us. He wants first of all to give us what is best for us—the gift of salvation. He will ask nothing of us that is not for His glory. If it is for His glory, it is for our good. We stand rewarded in eternity and joyful down here.

My friend, it is a good thing once in a while to think about your own death. I do not want to be morbid, but in what condition would you like to go out of this world? Where would you like to be? What would you like to have just done or what would you like to be doing when you pass into eternity? My friend, if you would like to do those things which please God in this life, what joy it will be in eternity! If in this life you are occupied with that which is selfish and empty and useless and of no eternal value, how is it going to be? We ought to pray that we will have an abundant entrance into the kingdom of God—that is, an entrance that comes laden with souls, with time well spent, with deeds done in His name, with a life lived for Him. His love to us is wonderful because we do not love Him instinctively, because there is nothing in us as sinners that is loving or lovely in the sight of a perfect God; but His love poured out all the blood in the veins of Jesus to wash us from our sins and to bring us into God's family. Oh, His love to us is wonderful.

Saul and the Witch of Endor

I Samuel 28:16

I want to tell you a story. There was a great evangelist who died just this side of the turn of the century. His name was Sam Jones. People sometimes say to me, "Was your father any kin to Sam Jones?" No, he wasn't. He never even met him. He lived down here in Georgia. He was a most interesting man. He was a drunken lawyer, and he got converted and God called him to preach. He was a rough and tumble kind of man. He preached a lot about judgment, made a lot of enemies, and won a lot of people to Christ.

One time he was conducting a meeting over in the city of Nashville, and a man came forward to find the Lord. While this man was being led to Christ, one of the preachers in the meeting came up and whispered in Mr. Jones's ear, "That man owns three riverboats. He is one of the meanest and richest men in this town." He got saved. He later built the Ryman Auditorium where the Grand Ole Opry used to be. It was built as a tabernacle—a fine, brick building. He built it so Mr. Jones would come back and hold another meeting. When you see that building practically abandoned now, you can remember it was built for the preaching of the gospel.

Captain Ryman said, "I want you to come to my home and meet my family." When they had time in the meeting, Mr. Jones went out to a great big, magnificent home. There were a number of men present in the living room, and he was introduced to them. Three of them he especially noted, as they were the three men who captained the boats that Ryman owned. The fourth man was the mayor of the city. As they were going into the dining room, Captain Ryman said aside to Mr. Jones, "I want to see these men get saved. I want you to go after them." They were seated two on one side and two on the other side of Sam Jones. All during the meal he dealt with them about their souls, but there was no response. He went away very heavy-hearted, but the last thing he said to the men was something like this, "God gives a man so many opportunities. It is dangerous to resist the wooing of the Lord's Spirit." He was gone from town only about six weeks or so when he had a letter saying that one of those captains had stepped on the deck of his ship and dropped dead of apoplexy. A few months later another man died in a similar fashion. Within six months, the third man died; and before the year was over, that mayor, as he was loading a shotgun, blew his head off.

You cannot resist God. You cannot resist God except at your peril. I am always worried when I preach. I would rather not preach than to preach without the anointing of God's Spirit upon me because somebody hearing the message, unless he is moved by it and turns to Christ, may be having his last opportunity to be saved. It happens. Sometime you will hear your last sermon. You are young people. I hope God, if the Lord tarries, will give you a long and useful life; but I hope it will be a life dedicated to Him and a happy life in Him. When I preach, I am always aware that somebody may hear me preach and resist the message, and I want to make the message so clear and so tender that no man can resist it because to resist the Holy Spirit is always a perilous thing to do. I think of students who have been here and heard the gospel message many times, who profess to be saved (and maybe they were) but who have never turned their lives over to God. God called them to certain tasks, asked for certain things, and they held back. Sometimes God has dealt with them in *this* life, and someday they are going to have to stand before God. Every one of us must give an account, and the greater our opportunities, the greater our obligations. The more chances we have to serve the Lord, the more we know about the Word of God, the more we learn about God's truth and God's grace, the more God expects of us. He gives us opportunities that we may be a blessing to other people. I would hate to think that somebody in these opening services has held back from God. I know there are some; but, my friend, I hope tonight, as you listen to this sermon, that God will move you to obey Him.

Our text is found in I Samuel 28:16. It is the only time in the Bible that a dead man speaks to a living man. There is an occasion in the New Testament where the Lord recounts a man in hell speaking to a man in paradise, but this is the one account where a dead man speaks to a living man. "Then said Samuel, Wherefore then dost thou ask of me, seeing the Lord is departed from thee, and is become thine enemy?" What an expression. It is bad enough to have the Spirit of the Lord removed from us, but for God to become our enemy is the most tragic thing that could happen in the life of any man—to have all the power of God's universe lined against you, the armies of heaven arrayed in military formation against you, and the might of God Himself turned against you.

Our scene opens. It is twilight time. A dejected man sits by a flickering campfire amidst the tents pitched on the side of a mountain. Burdened, heart heavy, his life as gloomy as the day that is settling down around him, he says to a friend, "The Lord has departed from me, and the Philistines make war against me. I have tried to find out from God how this is going to turn out, but He does not answer me by prophets or in any other fashion." Now, remember, this is Old Testament times, and God spoke through prophets in those days. He still speaks to us through the prophets as the record is written in the Word of God. Now that the record is finished and the Word of God completed, there is no further revelation. All the revelation we have of God's purpose and God's will is set down in this book. Now, God may talk to us sometimes if we are close to Him, applying some Scripture to something in our life. We may know of God's leading, but He always leads through the written Word of God and by the Word of God through the Holy Spirit.

Poor man. The head of the armies is in defeat, distressed, miserable. Why had God left him? Because he had disobeyed God. No man ever had a better start than Saul. He was tall, a head higher than any man in the kingdom. He was chosen by the people with God's consent to be their first king. He did not inherit a throne that had been corrupted by evil ancestry. He was the first of his line and the first king of Israel. For a little while he did wonderfully well. He was mighty in battle. He set a good example to his people, but the pride of kingship began to slip in upon him. Once God sent him off to do a job that was an unpleasant job. He was to go and kill all the Amalekites. Imagine. He was to wipe out a whole small nation and leave nothing alive—no man, no woman, no child, no suckling babe. All were to be wiped out forever.

Listen to me. Do not think God is cruel to do that. God had been merciful. He had passed this sentence upon them generations ago. He passed this sentence when they tried to hinder the people of God as they were coming into the land of promise. God had given them all these generations to repent. God, when He is angry, still remembers His mercy; but there has been no repentance. It is now time for the sentence of God to fall. God sometimes wipes out whole nations. God destroys cities, lands, and towns. If Bob Jones University ever departs from God's purpose, I hope He will destroy it. I would hate for this institution to remain here as just another educational institution with no sense of God's presence and no moving of His Spirit and no blessing of Almighty God upon it. That would be a terrible tragedy. But God was merciful to these wicked people who were corrupt with their sins, diseased because of their sins. How much better for those little babes to be slain and go out into eternity in innocence than to grow up and follow the sins of their parents and die and go to hell. Sometimes God is very merciful to take a little child.

Saul was to bring back nothing. He was to come back completely empty-handed, and God gave him a great victory. He is returning now triumphant. God sends the prophet out to meet him—the same prophet that He had used to give him the command to go. Saul talks so pious. Oh, how pious he can talk. "Thou man of God, I have done what the Lord told me to do." Just at that moment there were some sheep bleating and some cows mooing toward the back end of the train. The prophet said, "What means this lowing of the cattle in mine ear? God told you to kill them all. Apparently you brought some home." This man, this king, says, "The *people* brought them back. They want to sacrifice them to

God." Saul brought back the king too. He had not slain him with the rest. He wanted a prisoner, a trophy. The prophet said, "To obey is better than to sacrifice." Those cattle and sheep had not been brought back for sacrifice anyway. They had been brought back to breed with the king's herd. The prophet has them slain, and he himself takes the sword and cuts the king to pieces. He says to Saul, "God is going to depart from you. He will not speak to you any more." And he turned to leave him. The king laid hold on the prophet's mantle to pull him back, and the mantle ripped. Old Samuel said, "That is just the way the Lord is ripping your kingdom from you."

From that day until this night when we see Saul by the campfire in the gathering darkness, God has never spoken to him. It must be a terrible thing when God's man will not come to you with any message of grace, no word as to the moving of the Almighty, and when there is no sense in your life that God communes with you. Let me tell you, my friend, if you are saved and in sin, unconfessed and not made right with God, you will not have any communion with the Almighty except the voice of reproach as the Holy Spirit rebukes you for a while. God gives men time to repent, but eventually that rebuke will be silenced. You can never be used of God when there is unconfessed sin in your life, and you will never have any peace until you make things right with God.

Here Saul is—distressed, defeated. He said, "I have got to have an answer." When men do not look to God and find the answer in His Word, they are going to go to the wrong place for it. Don't think you ever need to go to some unsaved psychiatrist or some unsaved philosopher to find out what you need. The answer is always in the Word of God. But Saul says to one of his aides, "Can you find me somebody that has a familiar spirit?" But the king had just passed a law sometime before that anybody who dealt with the dead (witches, necromancers) should be put to death in the land. Strange, though, that this man knew of one. The order had not been carried out well. He replied, "There is a woman down here at Endor. They say she is pretty good at that sort of thing." The king said, "We will go down."

Imagine. What a humiliation for a mighty king. He puts on a disguise so he will not be recognized as royalty. I wonder what he found big enough to fit him in the camp, this tall king. He had to stoop his shoulders a little bit to find something that was long enough. Disguised and in the darkness, he descended from the hilltop down into the mist-filled valley. Listen. Sin always makes men dishonest. They disguise their deeds and pretend to be what they are not. They, who once stood erect, stoop. Seeking out the darkness, they go down. No sinner ever goes up. He may make money, but he is going down. A man called of God to preach the Word of God, if he becomes the richest man in the world in something else, has gone down from a high calling to an ordinary job. Men never get better in sin. Men always get worse. They say, "I am going to do this, but I am not going to let it master me. I will master *it*." By and by that thing you thought you had a hold on begins to hold *you*. It is always that way.

Since the Lord had departed from King Saul, he has become crazed, occasionally invaded by demons, a liar, a trickster, a breaker of promises, turning against David and making promises to him and then breaking them, seeking the life of those who are his servants. Always down. From royal nobility to bestial demonism. That is what happens. When you start turning away from God, you always set your face to darkness and your steps downward. It cannot be avoided. You say, "I am going to be the exception." If it weren't so tragic, I would laugh at you. *You* are going to be the exception? No man has ever been, and you are not big enough to beat the game of sin. No woman is, and no man is.

And they go in the darkness and come to a little house there on the edge of the village. It is a strange, half-buried, sod-covered house with a thatched roof. When they knock on the door, there is a shuffling inside and eventually the face of an old crone peeks out. "What are you coming for this time of night?"

The king, disguising his voice I am sure, said, "I want you to call up a dead man for me."

"You know that I cannot do that. King Saul has made that a death penalty. You are trying to catch me." The king swore nothing should happen to this woman, breaking his own law. They go into that little house. There are stuffed bats, snakeskins, and a smell of death in the place. "Whom do you want me to call up?"

"Call me up Samuel." For the first time in that woman's wicked career, God permits a dead man to come and speak.

Listen. When this is not trickery, this sort of thing is always demonic. If some demon pretends to be somebody whom you are seeking and you believe him, you will be led astray. God warns us to have nothing to do with these people who claim to commune with the dead. God for the first and last time permits a dead prophet to come back to an evil king. The woman, seeing who is there, turns and says, "You are King Saul. You deceived me."

The king says, "Do not worry. It is all right. What is he like?"

"Like gods coming out of the earth." Not one god but like gods. Apparently God had surrounded this man with a company of saintly dead spirits, an army of the dead in the house.

"What does he look like? The one I asked you to draw up."

"He looks like an old man in a mantle."

"It is Samuel. That is the prophet's mantle." It was like the one that Saul had rent that day when he tried to get God to change His mind and withdraw His sentence.

Then we hear from the mouth of this dead man, echoing around in this low-ceiling room. "Why do you ask of me? If God has departed from you and become your enemy, as much as I loved you and as proud as I was of you when I anointed you, as high as my hopes were for you, I am God's man. If God is your enemy, I am your enemy too." Listen, you cannot be a friend of God's enemies. Your heart can go out to them. You can try to reach them, but you cannot be the kind of friend with them that stoops to their acts and condones their doings. No sir. "Why do you ask of me? Do you expect me to tell you something that God does not tell you?"

83

Then the message comes. What a message! "Tomorrow by this time, you and all your sons will be with me. God is delivering your kingdom into the hand of the Philistines." Then he disappeared. What a message! The only message God has for the disobedient or unconverted person is an offer of grace and a sentence of death. The wages of sin—death. Thank God the gift of God is eternal life. The kingdom is divided. "It was prophesied long ago when you rent my robe, and it is being fulfilled now. The kingdom is going to fall, most of it, into the hands of the Philistines. You and all your sons in battle are going to die." Saul, who has not eaten, falls faint on the floor. This woman, demonic person that she is, feels so sorry for him that she insists he eat something. She has in the house with her (and that is interesting) a fatted calf. She kills it and dresses it and kneads dough and makes bread. The king is compelled to eat, so he starts his journey back in the strength of the food but in the weakness of God's curse.

Sad, isn't it? This man, appointed to a high place, did not just fail to obey something; but he set himself in pride against the Word of God. "I do not need to listen to God's Word. I can do as I please. I am above the Word of God. I am going to get by with the thing I am going to do, and God can like it or lump it." That was the attitude. That is a dangerous attitude to defy the Word of God, to shake your little fist in the face of the Almighty and say, "I *will*. I *must*. You *must* condone it." My friend, God is not a man. He cannot be threatened; He cannot be ignored; He cannot be disobeyed. Thank God, except to those who have sinned away their day of grace and hardened their hearts so much that God can no longer speak to them, unless God has withdrawn His Spirit as He withdrew it from Saul, there is always hope. God does remember mercy in the hour of wrath, and God gives to men an opportunity to make all things right as they confess their sins to Him. Sins confessed are cleansed, and sins turned from become a thing of the past, covered with the blood of Christ. The future ahead is clean.

I do not know who you are, but I know you are here. You know who you are, and you know I am talking right to you. You can go out of this place tonight with an old burden gone and that sense of fear that somebody will discover your past and that it will become known, removed. You can become a new creature in Christ Jesus, or you can be as a Christian restored to fellowship with God and again know the joy you once knew when you first trusted Christ before your sin and your will got in the way to mar the fellowship and darken your heart. Let us pray.

And Sitting Down
They Watched Him There
(Matthew 27:33-36)

Some men have been privileged to stand by at great events of history, to look on when the clock of time struck some special hour; but the crowd that was gathered outside the walls of Jerusalem the day of our Lord's crucifixion were present at an event marked red in the calendar of the ages. A strange crowd was there. Roman soldiers were going about the business of crucifying a man. There was nothing unique about that. Wherever Rome went, crosses crowned hilltops. Men were hung up to die. Some hung there for a week. It was the most cruel death man ever devised. There were hardhearted soldiers there with blood on their hands and blood on their souls—guilty, evil men. Then there was a mob, an ordinary crowd. The scum of the city gathered together to watch this cruel scene. They were bitter, howling, vicious. Some had been bribed by the priests to have a part in this. They are the ones who cried, "Release Barabbas and crucify Jesus." They have come out now to see the work completed.

The priests are there, robed in their ecclesiastical fringes and garments, with their phylacteries on their heads and their prayer shawls over their shoulders. They are the priesthood of organized religion. These men hate Christ because He challenged their privileges and rebuked their sinfulness and upbraided their greed. When they watch Him die, they say, "Well, isn't that nice. We will show Him who has the power in this land. It is not this teacher from Galilee but we who are the appointed men to head the religion of the land." You know, ecclesiastical leadership never changes. The worst ecclesiastical leadership always hates Jesus Christ because He challenges their claims, and they exercise power and take lordship over men. God does not decree that this should be.

There are some thoughtless ones in that crowd. There are always some thoughtless ones there. As they watch Him die, they do not understand at all what is going on. They think it is strange, perhaps, that a good man should be hung up to die between two thieves. They wonder why that could be, but they have no knowledge whatsoever that this is the fulfillment of the prophets who said long ago that his garments would be divided and that some would cast lots over them. These men had not read about the pangs of hell getting hold of Him and His being poured out like water and His bones being out of joint. The story in Isaiah 53 is being fulfilled. They just stand there and watch and, perhaps, have some sympathy and pity. They do not understand that this is God's plan for their redemption. No doubt a Roman senator was there with his purple-bordered toga falling in graceful folds about him. As he watched, he said, "My, how this speaks of Rome's universal power. Where Rome goes, she rules. If men stand contrary to Rome's advantages, they die. How wonderful this all is. Hail, Caesar."

Then there were some there who had known the miracles. Maybe some blind eyes had been opened, and they could see this cross because Christ had given them sight. Perhaps some had had crooked limbs straightened so they could make the little journey from Jerusalem out here. They watched Him die and thought, "Will it always be like this? Hate is strong, and love is weak, and good men die. He blessed me. He healed me. He has never done anything wrong. Why is He hanging there?" Those who had known His love and had walked with Him were in the crowd. Not close by, unfortunately, except for John. John and Mary, the mother, were standing nearby the cross. There somewhere in the outskirts of the throng were, possibly, some of those who had forsaken Him and fled when they took Him in the garden. They watched Him. Their conscience burned within them for forsaking Him. Oh, the tenderness with which they heard Him say to His mother, "Woman, behold thy son," and to the disciple, "Behold thy mother!" They marveled in that moment of suffering that He could remember the comfort of others.

Even His dying cry was misunderstood. *"Eli, Eli, lama sabach- thani?"* "My God, my God, why hast thou forsaken me?" They said, "He is a dying man. He is delirious. He is calling for a dead prophet." The blasphemous priest said, "Let's see if Elias will come and save Him." My friend, that is the saddest cry that ever echoed against heaven. "Why am I forsaken of God?" For the first time in all eternity, the Trinity is divided. Christ is made to be sin. God could not look on sin. For the first time He was separated, as we are separated, by our sins; but He had piled on Him all the sins of all the ages of every man and woman that ever lived and walked the earth. Did you ever stop to think that when He stood before Pilate and Pilate questioned Him, He could not profess innocence because He was made to be sin? All our guilt was on Him. He Himself, as the Son of God, was innocent of the charges. He, the Lamb of God, was guilty of them all, for our sins were laid on Him. So they watched. Human depravity made the cross necessary. It is because man is a depraved and lost creature that Jesus Christ, the pure and immaculate Son of God, had to die—the just for the unjust, the holy for the unholy, the righteous for the unrighteous.

This was the time for which He had come into the world. He said as He stood in the shadow of the cross, "For this was I born. For this hour came I into the world." He did not come just to do good deeds and teach men how to live. He came to die that men might have life. You misunderstand all the purpose of Christ if you look upon this as sort of an accidental ending, an unfortunate tragedy. No, my friend, this is the climax of all the ages—Christ's dying on a cross, shedding His blood that we may be free of sin. They watched *Him* there. They should have watched *us* there. If we got what was coming to us, we would be on that cross; but in His grace and in His mercy, they watched *Him* there. Who is this? This is the Rose of Sharon, the Bright and Morning Star; but the Rose is wilted, and the Star is eclipsed. This is the altogether Lovely One. As we see Him here, there is no beauty that we should desire Him. In fact, He looks more like a beast hanging up in the butcher shop. He hardly looks human. The joints are pulled apart. The bones are out of their sockets with the weight of His body on the cross. Isaiah had mentioned that too. His back is bruised and bleeding, cut by the soldiers' lashes in the night. His brow is crowned with thorns, and blood runs down and mingles with the blood from His beard where they plucked out the hairs in the night. His eyes are almost closed and are blackened by the fists of the soldiers. There He hangs. He hardly looks human. Indeed, He looks more like a victim than a man, but He is a man. He is God, the man. He is the victim of all our iniquity. In God's love and mercy, they watch Him there.

When I was a young man and knew less about human nature and human depravity, I wondered why men could turn on such a good man and do this; but the more I read about human nature, about wars and cruelty and torture and torment and prisons and inquisitions, the more I can understand it. Man is utterly and totally depraved. Maybe you say, "I would not have done that." Would you not? Anything any man ever did you are capable of doing. The most innocent of women and the most pure-hearted of men under the proper circumstances and the right temptations could commit any act that any monster in history has ever committed. What a picture this is of man's nature—not only of God's love but of man's hatred of God, of man's love for sin, of man's rejoicing in iniquity to watch Christ so punished. They watched Him there.

Only one man is converted. He is a thief suffering on a cross beside Him. I have often meditated on who this young thief might have been. Maybe he was the child of godly parents. Maybe he grew up in Galilee—maybe even in Nazareth. Maybe when he was a boy, he had heard stories of Jesus. I do not know. God lets us imagine things here so we can each put ourselves in his place. He is a thief, a murderer, an insurrectionist. Perhaps he listened to those who said, "You can be a hero. This is our land. We have a right to turn to violence to drive these Romans out." Corrupt priesthood is taking the tithe. "Let's get what we can. We are entitled to it. We will clean this land out." My friend, you can never "clean out" with filth. You only make things worse with filth and depravity and degeneracy. I do not know how he happened to be there, but he was hanging there.

On the other side is a thief somewhat older, apparently. Maybe he was the leader of the group or the lieutenant because Barabbas, who was the full leader, may have been in the crowd watching, since Christ had taken his place. The crowd asked for the thief and crucified the Savior, but one thief on the cross beside Him hears the fellow sufferer on the far side mock Him. "If you are the Son of God, come down from the cross. Save thyself and us." He turns and says, "Do you not fear God, seeing you are in the same judgment He is? We are here justly. We deserve what we are getting, but He does not deserve a thing." Then he turns toward the Lord and said, "Lord, remember me when thou comest into thy kingdom." Into the kingdom. That is glorious, but that kingdom is still not established on earth yet. How swift the mercy, how speedy the promise, how sudden the salvation—not in the kingdom but *that day* in paradise. The soul of a dying thief was the first little lamb of all the flock of God. When the Savior swept through pearly gates ajar, that little lamb was in His arms.

They watched Him there. We made that crown of thorns. We gathered those thorns on the barren hillsides of our godless hearts. We wove them into a crown when we denied Him His crown of glory. We pressed those thorns down upon His brow. Oh, the soldiers did it; but we did it too, for it is our sin that crowned Him with the thorns. We made the nails that were driven in His hands. We mined the ore down in the dark galleries of our filthy thoughts. We fired it on the fires of our lusts, and with the hammers of our rejection, we shaped the nails. We drove them in His palms and in His feet. We pierced Him. We made the cross.

Did you ever think what that cross might have been? It might have been the mast of a tall ship sailing in blessing across the seas in service for mankind. It could have been the rafter of a little house to shelter a family from the storms and snows of winter. But it was a cross. It was a cross we fashioned of the gifts that God has given us. We deny His sovereignty and put His gifts to the use of our own pleasure and our own sinful wishes. I have often wondered: Did Christ ever stop under a tree some day when the sun was hot and the disciples were tired and, as He sat there, look up and say, "This is the one." He knew. Did you ever stop to think what a sad thing it was for that tree to become a cross? He let the seed fall in the ground. He sent the rain to water it and the sun to warm it. The shoot came up, for He is the maker of all things. He sent the winds from the western sea to blow upon it and make it strong and straight. He sat, perhaps, under its shade one day and said, "This is the cross." It is a cross we fashioned, and our sin nailed Him to that cross.

They watched Him there. Satan always tries to turn our gaze elsewhere. You see the babe in the manger. Everybody says, "Isn't that a beautiful sight? Look at the sweetness of the childhood and the care of the mother." Nobody says, "Child of Bethlehem, come out of the manger." There is no salvation in the child. There is sweetness there and promise but nothing more. We see Him touching blind eyes to make them see. We say, "Look at the wonder of these miracles." Nobody ever said, "Cease from working miracles, Great Physician." We hear His words of wisdom, the bluntness of His speech, His rebuke of sin. We listen to the loveliness of the Sermon on the Mount. Nobody says, "Come down from the hillside, Great Preacher." The cry is always, "Come down from the cross." Men hate the cross because the cross shows them up as they are. Men do not like to recognize they are sinners. We have students here, I am afraid, like this. "I am not so bad." You are bad enough to go to hell. "I am not so wicked." You are wicked enough to offend a holy God by your thoughts and lies and deeds and ambitions and lusts. The cry is still, "Come down from the cross." When we see Him on the cross, we see Him for the purpose of His coming. Without that cross, hell would be fuller and heaven would be empty of any redeemed.

They watched Him there. It is when we look on the cross that we see ourselves as we are and see God as He is and see our hope of heaven. We should be touched to serve Him, for He gave Himself for us. He gives us salvation full and free. We cannot earn it, we cannot buy it, we cannot steal it. His blood must be all our plea. A perfect plea. The availing blood, the cleansing blood, the precious blood, the preserved blood, the blood in God's presence where the great company of angels and the church of the first-born are gathered in the presence of God the Father—that blood with a thousand tongues and each one saying, "Father, forgive. I shed this blood that they may be guiltless and come into Thy presence as sons and daughters of God." That blood cries out as Abel's blood never could—more perfectly, for Abel's blood speaks of vengeance, death, and murder. His blood speaks of murder a thousand times worse and death a hundred times more pitiful. That blood speaks of salvation, and that blood pleads for us. We who know its cleansing power should hold back nothing from Him.

They watched Him there; and God, looking down from heaven, watches us where we are and sees in our life something He wants, something He needs (if I may put it that way). The wonderful thing is that God needs men to serve Him and women to glorify Him. Angels cannot preach the gospel. Angels cannot talk to sinners about their need of salvation, but we who have tasted and seen how good the Lord is have an eternal obligation as well as a lifetime obligation. As long as He gives us breath, that breath should be used to talk about Him. As long as we have strength, that strength should be expended in His service. All we have belongs to Him, for we are not our own. We are bought with a price; and, oh, what a price—the precious blood of Jesus. Thank God He died for us. Where would we be without that cross? What hope would we have without that blood? All we can do is say, "Here I am."

> When I survey the wondrous cross,
> On which the Prince of glory died,
> My richest gain I count but loss,
> And pour contempt on all my pride.
>
> See, from His head, His hands, His feet,
> Sorrow and love flow mingled down;
> Did e'er such love and sorrow meet,
> Or thorns compose so rich a crown?

This crown demands our soul, our life, our all. Will you say, "*Shall* have my soul, my life, my all"? Let us pray.

Remembrances

Remembrances

*The following pages contain reminiscences and remembrances
of Dr. Bob Jones Jr. by friends, acquaintances, colleagues, and
graduates. Some were written to Dr. Jones before his passing.
Others were written to the family after his passing.*

His Preaching Ministry

Cal Mair

In August 1972 I began my freshman year as a Bible major. It
was during my first Bible conference when your dad preached the
message "I AM THAT I AM" that I realized how much his life
would affect mine. I sat there listening to every word as he painted
a picture in my mind that I would never forget. Here was a man
who was truly in love with the God that he served. I began to look
forward to the times when he would return to campus and speak in
chapel and the Sunday morning services. I would write to him for
advice, and he would always answer. He cared for each one of us.

After I graduated and began my ministry here at The WILDS,
one of my fondest memories was when your dad was here for the
week and he wore his Pittsburgh Steelers jersey all around the
campsite. It seemed so strange to see him without a coat and tie on!
On one occasion he even came into the kitchen and chatted with
me concerning food service and your mom's involvement in teaching foods courses there at the University. He really was interested
in what I was doing here for the Lord.

Now my son Jeremy is a sophomore at BJU. I am so glad he
was able to sit under the ministry of your dad, even if it was for a
short time.

Dr. Bruce D. Cummons

Back in the midseventies I invited your dad to be with us for a one-week revival meeting. Those were days of great victory . . . and Massillon Baptist Temple was often reaching attendances around the two thousand mark. The battle was on concerning the KJV.

When writing to Dr. Bob, I enclosed a little "one-liner request" that we enclose in all of our letters of invitation to speakers who were coming to minister to us. [It said,] "Dr. Jones, we ask all of our speakers to preach from and read from the KJV when in our pulpit. Because of the battle today, we do not want to further confuse our people here at Massillon Baptist Temple." A note came from his secretary to the effect that Dr. Jones always used the KJV in his meetings, which I, of course, already knew.

It was probably the third night of the meeting that I noticed something. Your dad would announce his text or a passage of Scripture he would use in the message; and while we were looking down at our Bibles, he would quote the passage of Scripture word for word! I began "peeking" each evening, and invariably he would quote the portion he was to preach from! I was impressed and humbled by this precious man of God. Our fellowship was sweet; and though a great and good man and a genuine scholar, when we were together, he was as humble and common as any preacher I've ever met.

Rev. Jesse Bobo

As you preached the sermon for the Praise Service Thursday morning and reminisced about your father's being at his best on special occasions like Thanksgiving and funerals, my mind went back to the funeral of Harold Kilpatrick. It was the most emotionally charged funeral I had ever been to. In addition to Brother Harold's family and congregation, there were many preachers there to whom Brother Harold had been a mentor and father figure. The sanctuary was filled with audible sobs until Dr. Bob Jr. stood to speak. Within minutes a hushed peace had come over that whole place and all who were there. I have never forgotten that experience, and I have commented to others many times of how God mightily used Dr. Bob to comfort on that occasion.

Dr. Greg McLaughlin

Recently I was in Colorado on an elk hunt. I hunted in a grove of aspens. In the middle of the grove stood a huge old aspen. It was battered and scarred with age, but it was yet strong and beautiful. The wind that day was unbelievable (40-50 mph gusts). I heard what I thought were gunshots but later realized were aspen trees snapping in the wind and falling to the forest floor. As the wind grew stronger, I watched one tree get caught by the wind, begin to move in a circular motion, then snap and fall. Then another and another. But the old aspen stood strong. I decided I would get away from some of the smaller trees, and no sooner than I did, the very tree I was leaning on began to swirl and then crack and pop, and it too came crashing down. But the old aspen stood.

As I watched the grove of trees, my thoughts of seeing an elk were crowded out by the plight of the aspens. Then the thought hit me. These trees are like today's preachers. They get caught by every wind of doctrine, begin to move in all directions, and then come crashing down. And when I thought of it and even some preachers I know personally who don't stand where they used to, my heart broke. Then I looked, and the old aspen stood strong against the force of the wind, and I said to myself, "That old aspen is like Dr. Bob Jones Jr., battered and scarred by the fight of Faith but still standing." What an inspiration! I thank God for his stand and for his love for preachers.

Mr. and Mrs. Scott Gembola

I will always remember your father not just for his wonderfully eloquent sermons but for his continual stand against compromise. His stand has greatly helped us over the years as we had to make decisions on where to attend church. I feel God has greatly blessed us because we didn't compromise.

Dr. Robert V. Warren

What an honor and privilege to know your father! Though always taking a firm biblical stand on the fundamentals of the Faith, which liberals and the New Evangelical camp misinterpreted as "lack of love and fundamental hardness," he was to those who had the privilege of knowing him and his heartbeat, a man of tenderness, kindness, and love.

Mrs. Jim Roschi

Perhaps it would be comforting for you to know the impact your loved one made on our extended family.

In the late 1940s or early 1950s, Dr. Bob was in the audience of a Billy Graham crusade in Los Angeles. Billy Graham became ill as he began his message, and he said that although he didn't feel up to preaching the message, there was a gentleman on the front row very capable of preaching it for him. My dad tells how Dr. Bob came to the platform, put a New Testament on the corner of the pulpit, and without any notes began preaching one of the most powerful sermons my dad had ever heard. Through the preaching of the Word, my parents, Al and Roberta Mast, came to Christ.

Shortly thereafter, the Masts invited Roberta's parents to come to church. Both Tom and Ruby Wagner were also gloriously saved. Thomas Wagner was a very influential man politically in the Gardena, California, area. People were amazed to see the complete transformation in his life. Al and Roberta's two daughters also came to Christ as a result of their parents' decision. Their oldest daughter, Susan, attended Bob Jones University, and I graduated from the school a few years later. Although I was reared in a Christian home, it was during an opening meeting of my junior year in college where Dr. Bob was preaching that I received assurance of my salvation. It was also at the University where I met my husband. Today the Lord has given us a wonderful ministry at Colonial Hills Baptist Church where we serve under a Bob Jones University graduate. We have had the opportunity to steer many, many young people down to the University over the years. We now have three children of our own, all of whom have trusted Christ as their Savior and plan to attend Bob Jones University.

Rev. T. Lee Hendricks

My heart is thrilled to have been under [Dr. Bob Jr.'s] and your influence, not only as a student but subsequently as a pastor. I will always recall a message your father preached in Bible Conference in either 1977 or 1978 about Saul and the witch of Endor. The Shakespearean overtones in the message were so vivid that if one closed his eyes, he could see the wart on the witch's nose and smell the fire and hear her cracking voice speaking to this hulk of a man, Saul. From the moment he took the podium to the close of the message, there was such an anointing of the Lord on your father that gripped my heart. I knew, as the Lord called me to preach, that kind of clarity and unction was what I desired.

[Dr. Bob] certainly will be remembered as one of the giants of our faith. A man of courage, tenacity, and abiding faith in our heavenly Father which led him through many years of building a legacy which will stand as a testimony of what God can do in the life of a dedicated servant. I'm sure that many, with much more eloquence, will speak of their reflections on this man of God, but I know that I am greatly indebted to him and to you for the part you have had in building my foundation on the solid Rock.

J. Dwight Anderson

My father was saved as a young man in Tom Malone's church in Pontiac, Michigan. For whatever reason, he drifted and did not live for the Lord during the following several years. When he was thirty-five years of age, he began listening to Bob Spencer on a radio broadcast in Huntsville, Alabama, and we eventually began attending his church, where I was saved in April of 1968 as a thirteen year old. Shortly after we began attending, your father preached a week of messages at the church. . . . On several occasions my father spoke of that week of messages. He recounted how that every night your father spoke on an issue that my father was struggling with. He thought Dr. Bob had planned each night just for him. He considered that week a watershed in his spiritual life—a life which subsequently touched many people and led many into the kingdom of God. As you might expect, my father thought the world of your father.

Dr. Bud Bierman

One alumni pastor in Michigan told me about Dr. Bob's speaking for their church banquet. As he sat at the head table, he realized the theme of the evening was "pearls." He took a napkin and jotted down some thoughts while he was eating. He then got up and preached a marvelous message on "The Pearl of Great Price," with biblical passages and interesting facts about pearls. Some of the people seated near him saw him prepare this "on-the-spot" outline and never forgot it.

Dr. Bob's ability to develop a message on the spot was legendary. I experienced this firsthand one Sunday morning when I was presiding for the service here on campus. Dr. Bob had given me a Scripture portion from Daniel to read. He got up and preached a masterful sermon from that portion. After the service, with a twinkle in his eye, he said, "You threw me a curve this morning." When I asked him why, he said, "You read the wrong passage!" In the short time between the Scripture reading and the time for him to get up and preach, he prepared a message from the portion I had read.

Dr. Ken Hay

One of the most memorable services I attended during all the years I was at Bob Jones University was one of the opening night revival meetings when Dr. Jones preached his message on David and Bathsheba. At the end of the message, he did not have any music but just gave an invitation for people to come. I do not know when I have been in a service where there was such a holy hush over the congregation and such a strong moving of the Spirit of God. Students poured into the counseling rooms to make things right with God. I learned during that service that you do not have to have hype or even music but only the power of God upon His Word to see hearts broken, souls saved, and Christians challenged to be more like Christ.

Dr. Thurman Wisdom

So many have spoken of Dr. Bob's eloquence that I hesitate to speak of it, but there is a dimension of his power to communicate that should not be overlooked. His was not a contrived eloquence.

I heard a preacher once who advertised far and wide that he spent an hour in preparation for every minute he spoke in public. He had a reputation for being eloquent; but his messages came across as fluffy and flowery, and they had no lasting effect. Dr. Bob's eloquence always seemed to rise from the depths of his soul. Because his messages came from the depths of his soul, they reached deep into the heart; and, I might add, his eloquence was enhanced as much by what he did not say as it was by what he did say. In the forty-five years that I had the opportunity of hearing Dr. Bob preach publicly and speak privately, I cannot remember a single incident in which he promoted himself or his accomplishments. His was a true eloquence in that his highest objective was to communicate the message that was on his heart.

Dr. Bruce McAllister

As a boy I remember Dr. Bob's coming to our church in Alabama. At the beginning of his message, he asked us to turn in our Bible to some rather obscure Old Testament passage. For some reason I looked up while he was "reading" the passage. I was amazed that Dr. Bob was looking out at the audience quoting the obscure passage from memory. I believe that he did this type of thing often in those days.

Mrs. Ralph Ingersoll

We heard of the loss of your father with sorrow. Not only will the University miss him but also the nation at large. His wonderful Christian work and impact on people's lives cannot be measured. We will always cherish the times that we had the privilege to hear him speak, the last of which incidentally was last Mother's Day in Raleigh, North Carolina. It was my Mother's Day present from Shaun and Deborah to take us to hear Dr. Bob. Ralph commented at the time that this was a special joy because we did not know when such an opportunity would come again. Dr. Bob, your father did not use one note. He opened his Bible and gave us the reference, but he quoted the passage from memory, as he had done so many times before. His message, as always, was timely and powerful.

A journey successfully run, he has finished his course triumphantly; and we now rejoice with him as he is welcomed to his eternal home to be forevermore with his Lord and Savior that he lovingly served all these years.

Rev. Dick Brady

What can I add to many thousands of words that have been expressed to you in your loss? Perhaps one thing that I will always cherish was his personal graciousness to me each time he was with us. He seemed to preach with as much fervor here (a small work) as I heard him in larger audiences. Although he was my college president who instilled within me biblical principles and convictions, as an adult, I always felt he was my personal friend. He always seemed to have time for me—and that meant a lot to me in the discouragements of a small work. We will not forget him.

Second Samuel 1:25a ("How are the mighty fallen in the midst of the battle") has come to mind. By [Dr. Bob's] example and steadfastness and by God's grace, it will be a little easier to keep the faith as we continue in "the battle." Your dad has laid his armor down; our ministry is to "continue on" as he so often exhorted us.

Rev. Wade Kuhlewind

Several have come, a number of preachers, friends of the University too. Everyone has now left. It's a few minutes after broadcasting your father's funeral service from the Internet. It was such a moving service. Your dad was not canonized or beatified, but the Lord Jesus was lifted up. What more could he have desired than for the Lord Jesus to get all the glory due His Name?

Your dad is greatly beloved here. His preaching here for evangelistic meetings is not forgotten. Honestly, folks still speak of his gospel message preached in November of 1989. No one has ever heard a more clear presentation of the gospel and clear appeal to receive Christ. I wrote in a church newsletter that your dad was often misunderstood and the media only played one side of his multifaceted life. We know better.

Lt. Commander Patrick Doney

(Written to Dr. Jones after the diagnosis of his illness)

Although I was never able to let you know this before, I wanted to tell you that if there were a preacher I looked forward to hearing, it was you. You inspired me. I was impressed with your spirituality, enjoyed your humor, and, just in general, I enjoyed hearing you preach the Word of God. It was always a pleasure to hear that you were going to be the speaker—whether it was chapel or Sunday morning worship service in the Amphitorium or a meeting or fellowship dinner in some other place.

For the twenty years I was a U.S. Navy chaplain, you encouraged me and made me feel like you were a friend of my ministry (while I had many adversaries who did not appreciate me or my background). When I was around you, I felt like you were my friend, and it helped me all the way. I wanted to thank you for that.

My wife and I both greatly respect and appreciate your ministry and encouragement and all that you did to make BJU the great place it is. Your cultural and creative touch will continue for the benefit of Christian young people until Jesus comes again.

Dr. William Raymond

The first time I ever saw Dr. Bob Jones Jr. was on September 5, 1956 (my eighteenth birthday). My father had dropped me off at Bob Jones University that afternoon, and I was sitting in the Rodeheaver Auditorium. It was the opening evangelistic service of the new school year. Dr. Bob did not preach that night—his father did—but I recall how impressed I was with the dignified way he presided over the service, and I still remember some of the things he said as he welcomed the students. I developed an admiration for him that night, and I have admired him ever since.

I admired his preaching. Without question, he was my favorite preacher. He was an orator in the pulpit. Someone has said that "he had the polished, well-educated approach, with a voice that flows like ripples of water in a clear running mountain stream." He had memorized many passages of Scripture, and as a boy, he memorized the entire Methodist hymnal to please his grandmother.

I admired the fact that he was one who had an interest in many fields. He lived up to the old adage that he altered slightly: "Be a jack-of-all-trades, but a master of *one*." In reality, he was a master of *many*—evangelist, educator, scholar, administrator, architect, poet, Shakespearean actor, and connoisseur of the arts. His contribution to the development of Bob Jones University is immeasurable.

I admired him for his faithfulness to the Word of God and for his defense of the Faith. He grew up with the Fundamentalist movement. The University his father founded was started in the midst of the Fundamentalist-Liberal controversy to give young people the opportunity to receive a Christian education. It is quite possible that Dr. Bob knew personally more of the leaders of Fundamentalism than any other man. He never wavered in his stand for the Bible, the Book that he loved more than any other.

Finally, I admired him for his love and concern for preachers, including this unworthy preacher. When he stepped down as president of Bob Jones University in June of 1971, he stated that he wanted to spend the rest of his life helping preachers and missionaries. That he did right up until his illness laid him aside a few months ago.

Vyacheslav Starikov

I am a former Timothy student. I arrived late to school because of some visa problems, and I remember when I first heard Dr. Bob. I had many fears then about the school because I didn't know much about it. My way to school was full of testings, but as I heard his preaching against sin and for holiness in each believer's life, I felt that I was in a safe place spiritually. His sober manner and vivid preaching left an impact that I still clearly remember. I am studying in grad school now and am very grateful to the Lord for this place of training for my future ministry in Russia.

Robert Harlan

Though I am only a freshman here at BJU, I feel as if Dr. Bob is a part of me. There will never be another person like him. His wisdom astounded those who heard him preach, and even at his ripe old age, he was upbeat, creative, and very humorous. He never lost his sense of humor, even to the end. His excellent taste and appreciation for the fine arts have helped make BJU what it is today. I am glad I made it here when I did, just in time to see Dr. Bob before he passed into realms of glory and to understand a part of why BJU is what it is today—a university a step above the rest and a beacon of light and truth in an age of darkness. May his life be an example to all of us—a life lived for Christ and a faith that stood strong, even to the very end.

Rev. Scott Wiedeman

I will never forget the honor your father bestowed upon me by fitting my church's Mortgage Burning Service into his schedule. He was so kind to fly and ride all the way out to Walla Walla, Washington, to preach for this then-new pastor five years ago. I felt very privileged to be able to spend some time with him during that weekend. . . . He certainly has meant a lot to me, and I will miss him.

Rev. David Nash Sr.

I want to share some thoughts with you about your dad when he was here to preach at First Baptist of Troy in late September. I sat in the third pew from the front and observed him very closely. We sang some of the old majestic hymns of the faith that day, and your dad stood up without a hymnal in his hand and sang *every* word of each hymn from memory. He knew those hymns by heart even down to the fifth stanza.

After the morning message he stayed by the pulpit area, so I went up to chat with him. I told him I was a member of Bryan Society. He informed me that he had started that society back in Cleveland. Though he looked a little pale, I told him we were glad to see him. Then he told me he had to see the doctor on Monday morning to find out the results of some tests. That evening he preached his second sermon on the demons of Gadara. He preached his heart out, though only for thirty minutes. Pastor Harding had mentioned to our congregation that you didn't want him to come on that trip because he was so sick. I'm glad you relented because he was a real blessing to our people.

Dr. Norman Marks

I got to know your dad when I became a banquet chairman; after that we hit it off well. He was kind enough to tolerate my earthy nature. He was a spiritual father to so many. I had a tremendous dad, so I looked to Dr. Bob Jr. as an elder shepherd who had great wisdom and powerful discernment bred of a biblical knowledge. He was an ambassador of good will to all who love God and God's Book. He was firm but never hard-boiled. We preachers of the Fundamentalist heritage knew he was our friend even as he led us. He brought culture to the Fundamentalist ranks. God knows Fundamentalists need that! I feel so blessed to have had him as a friend.

Michelle Lewis

I will always remember the way he spoke to us in chapel as if we were family, not just students. He encouraged us, scolded us, and shared memories with us just as a grandfather would. It was so plain to see that he loved us. I'll never forget when he came out of the cake with a huge hat on his head at the end of Faculty Body on Gold Rush Daze and then looked around in amazement as if he couldn't figure out why everyone was laughing so hard. He always had fun!

Dr. Earl Nutz

I appreciated your father. His consistent preaching of the gospel over the multitude of years encouraged those of us who do our teaching of the Bible in the classroom. He never quit. He never changed his message. He always showed his concern for the truly important things of this life. He never lost his singular focus on serving the Lord. He was a great example to all of the faculty.

I also appreciated your father's emphasis on the Bible rather than on some theological system. Bob Jones University is spiritually stronger because of that emphasis. You would be surprised how often we in the Bible Department talk about the matter of having a truly Bible-centered emphasis here. We owe your father a debt of gratitude for his part in maintaining that emphasis over the years.

Dr. Marshall Neal

I was a student in Cleveland when Dr. Bob first taught homiletics. He continued to teach it and eventually wrote the book used for many years, *How to Improve Your Preaching.* After it was published, I heard him say jokingly he wanted to name it *Preaching: And How!*

One memory from the class [is of] a discussion of the introduction of the sermon. He surprised us by saying that a sermon's introduction should be like a woman's evening dress: suggestive but not revealing. For a long time I felt that the best part of his sermons was his interesting introductions.

He would assign verses for the class to make outlines for sermons. I still remember some of those assignments. Shortly after our class turned in the assignment on Revelation 21:1 ("And there was no more sea"), he preached a sermon on it. We accused him of taking our sermon, but he protested that he already had the ideas for the message. Of course, his sermon was far better than ours. We were assigned to make three outlines on Philippians 3:10, "The power of his resurrection, and the fellowship of his sufferings, being made conformable unto his death." That was a difficult assignment with such a short portion of Scripture to work on. The outlines which I prepared were instrumental in carrying me through the following summer of preaching each week to the same people.

Other factors which shaped my life and preaching are the memorizing and use of hymns in sermons as well as matching hymns to be used in the service with the subject he planned to preach on so the audience would be thinking along that line when he began to preach.

To give one illustration of his use of language, the last time I was on the platform with him to lead in prayer, he preached on "The Disobedience of Saul and the People" (I Sam. 15). He described them as "a caravan of compromise."

His Influence

Rev. Mike Felber

My memories from childhood go back to the time when your father came in the mid-1960s to help our church in Indianapolis. Those revival meetings were not only a benchmark for our church but were also influential in my life as an eight-year-old. He took time to encourage me. From that time he was one of my heroes.

We appreciate the faithfulness that your family has demonstrated in doing what God called you to do. As each one has been promoted to God's reward ceremony, another family member has stepped in to "keep on keeping on."

Rev. George Youstra

When I became a pastor and took on an established denomination to make my church independent, Dr. Bob was there for me when so many others didn't have the time. I will always remember that. Praise the Lord for a man who practiced what he preached.

Dr. Robert Lair

I always felt rather close to [Dr. Bob], though my only opportunities to be very close came when I understudied his Macbeth, Shylock, and Richard II with the drama department there at BJU. It was a thrill to me to be so close to such an extraordinary human being.

In my own history, four of my five brothers and sisters never finished high school. My father had really rathered I not go to college. He urged me to stay at home and get a job. (We were a very poor Depression family.) One summer day at the end of my senior year of high school, I dogged your father down in a cemetery adjacent to a Presbyterian church in Schenectady, New York (the one that gave the mosaic of the angel of inspiration to the University). He was thirty-nine at the time, I believe. The result of that conversation was that I knew I must enroll at BJU. And I did, struggling to pay even the generously small tuition and fees then in effect.

That decision was surely the most important one of my entire life. And your father was always the source of great encouragement to me, both then and in more recent years. I keep and treasure several very kind and very encouraging letters he sent me over the years. I know his memory, his influence upon many lives, lives on and that mine is just one instance of his enduring and decisive ministry to many over the years.

Mrs. Richard Horak

We had been praying for your dad each day in our home school. I had the privilege of meeting your father for the first time last January while on campus with my husband. I told him our meeting was "the highlight of my visit." I and our two youngest sons got to sit with him for a few minutes and chat. I told him we were praying for all ten of them to graduate one day from BJU. With that he reached in his pocket and pulled out a dollar for each of them—it was their first down payment for BJU he said.

Donna Hess

I'm sure that you have received myriad cards and letters recounting anecdotes about your dad. I suppose anecdotes are the best way for those of us who knew him to celebrate his life. Ours are, of course, only bits of cloth compared to the richer tapestry of your memories. Still, they are part of the whole, and sharing them is our way of letting you know how much we loved him.

The first time I ever spoke to your dad we talked of books, a seemingly insignificant topic—but not to me. I was in my early teens, unsaved, and recently enrolled in Bob Jones Academy. The circumstances for my coming to the University were unusual, and to say that I was not a typical Academy student would be an understatement. When I arrived on campus I had no understanding of the gospel, no knowledge of Scripture, no family, no Christian friends or acquaintances. Indeed, campus life was so antithetical to my experience that I had decided my only option was to leave. Before I could implement my plans to leave, however, I received a call from your dad's secretary. He had a question and wanted me to stop by his office after chapel. The question pertained to a minor legal issue and was quickly dispatched. He then turned the conversation, asking me what I liked to do in my spare time. I mentioned reading, and we spent the next half-hour talking of authors and books, of heroes and villains. It was the first time since my arrival that I felt at all at ease. I left his office that morning still unsaved, still uncertain, but willing to wait a little longer.

Now nearly thirty years have passed, and as you know, *much* has changed. Still, I often think about that morning when God used your father to build a bridge for me from one life to another. We had our last conversation in the Blue Room [of the Dining Common] in late October. (I was baby-sitting your grandchildren.) As may be guessed, your dad and I talked of books. I find it hard now to say good-bye to one I wish could always be there and impossible to give due tribute to one who meant so much. So I will close with a line from Caesar that has been much upon my mind since that Wednesday morning: "Friend, I owe more tears / To this dead man than you shall see me pay. / I shall find time. . . . I shall find time."

Luena Barker

Your father always made me feel I could do things when I felt so inadequate. Years ago he asked me to take the [Administrative] Conference minutes because the secretary was needed in her office at that time; and when I explained that I knew no shorthand, he said, "Just do the best you can," and he put up with my trying to do that job for several years until they had a secretary who could be spared at Conference time.

He always encouraged me in the summers when I went to Winona Lake [to represent the University] by kindly suggesting how we could improve our display, etc. Because he seemed to have confidence in me, I was determined to try to do everything he asked me to do. No wonder I loved and admired him as so many others did.

Edith Markham

During the fifty-seven years I knew Dr. Bob, I observed him as a father, an actor, an educator, and a preacher of the gospel. My conclusions are from one saved because of the ministry of a Bob Jones student, trained at Bob Jones when the school was in Cleveland, Tennessee, and employed as a teacher in the Academy for fifty-three years.

The first photograph I took when I arrived on campus was of Dr. Bob and his young son Bob Jones III. From that day until the opening of school this fall, I have appreciated the loving teamwork of those two.

No one could make Robert Browning's poetry live like Dr. Jones. Everybody thinks of Dr. Bob as a Shakespearean actor; I'll always remember his "Curtain Calls," special appearances on Vespers and concerts, and his roles in films.

Saying much in a few words is a gift all educators need. Whether Dr. Bob was at an opening meeting of the school year or giving instructions at a faculty meeting, he was rhythmically epigrammatic. He always had biblical goals for the school and worked toward those milestones.

Of all the memories I have of Dr. Bob, the dominant picture is of his preaching at chapel or during a Sunday morning service. The imagery, the warmth, and the urgency of his message were unique. Having traveled in the Middle East, he had seen many of the places about which he spoke, a situation that added to his sermons.

Doris Harris

From terror born of awe and admiration to a friendship based on those same qualities, Dr. Bob Jones Jr. was part of our lives for nearly fifty years.

He wasn't like a grandfather to our family. Dr. Bob Sr. was that. Dr. Bob Jr. was, rather, like an exciting uncle whose zest darted into and out of our lives; who traveled to faraway places and whose presence of conviction, energy, artistry, humor, and kindness glimmered into and over our lives, illuminating them like a powerful lighthouse ray. He was always the dashing Cyrano with his white plume that symbolized his honor (my first play with him, when I was a sophomore).

Wherever Dr. Bob walked, there was zest and excitement. He was home from Europe; home from the Middle East; home from Ireland with new stories to tell and new convictions to share. When he saw something wrong, he wanted it fixed. When he saw an error, he wanted it corrected. When he visited a rehearsal, he wanted things to be just right. Sometimes when changes were made with great difficulty, it was hard to admit that he was *always* right about the details. In fact, at times it was downright disgusting at *how right* he always was. His eye for detail in a production was unerring. Much of the credit for the success of our major productions was due to his sacrifice of time to make sure all was well. Conviction and energy and artistry always followed in his wake. They were rays that emanated from the lighthouse of his life. They reflected his white plume of honor.

How he could preach the Word! What a grasp of language. We walked the dusty roads of the Holy Land and felt the joy of the woman with the issue of blood as she touched His garment. We chuckled at the scene of Peter leaving his beloved boat. With his trained voice and eloquence and masterful knowledge of the language, and more importantly of the Word, he brought an eloquence to the pulpit that is seldom seen in this generation.

He brought such beauty into our lives. Growing up on campus, my children begged to spend nearly every Sunday afternoon at the Art Gallery; later as student workers they worked there. How that enriched all of our lives. The fine arts were part of everyday life. Every graduate is richer because of him. Our fine arts emphasis and department, to which I've given my life, is a gift of the Founder's vision brought into life by this multitalented Renaissance man, Dr. Bob Jones Jr.

I don't know at what point he changed from administrator, to beloved uncle, to friend. But it happened largely through his sense of humor. How he teased. He had a most unique sense of humor. I was so shy and in awe of him that it took me years to realize that his teasing revealed his disdain for those who took themselves too seriously, and he loved it when you could "give and take" with him. During one production I was sobbing over his "dead body" as he lay there—making jokes. During a curtain call I was beside him when he moved forward, and with a most gracious smile took his bow while out of the side of his mouth he said, "They're just being polite; it's not genuine applause."

He frequently stopped at the table with the newest joke. I often thought and truly believe that some of his enemies just didn't understand how much he liked a good joke and often couldn't tell when he was joking and when he was serious. We had a long visit with him the Saturday before he went in to be diagnosed on Monday. He wasn't feeling great, but he still had a joke to tell and a laugh to share and an eagerness to preach in my home state, Michigan, the next day.

I had been told he didn't like cats, so I put our cat in our library when he was a guest in our home. We didn't want him bothered by its presence. We lost Dr. Bob. I searched the house for him. He was in the library having an absolutely great time playing with the cat.

One of the kindest men I ever knew, he took great care to hide his generous heart. Like Cyrano, he was tough and tender. He was shy about others knowing about his tender and generous side. He gave financial help to an old, retired faculty member no longer with the school. Chairs were donated to our little struggling mission church in Georgia. Hymnbooks were given to our little country church in South Carolina. He arranged for faculty men who were pastors to take a dreamed-of Holy Land trip. My husband was one of them. He preached in our little church and blessed hearts of our small congregation on pastor-appreciation day. Deep down Dr. Bob was a tender and sensitive man. One sure proof of this was his choice of selections in his collection of favorite poems. I would not have known of these tender, never-advertised acts of kindness had we not been directly involved. We are just two of the Bob Jones University family. Undoubtedly there were hundreds, if not thousands, of other such acts.

It has always been my contention that God's greatest gift to this earth is a man who is in every way masculine and a fighter for his faith, who at the same time has unique sensitivity. They are not often found in the general population. My husband is one. Many of the men in our Bob Jones University family are such men. Dr. Bob Jones was definitely such a man.

And always beside him, or behind him, or waiting and praying for him was his beautiful, gracious, soft-spoken wife. He could never have been what he was had she not been what she is.

In the play *Cyrano de Bergerac,* whose character Dr. Bob played so beautifully, Cyrano is concerned that he die with his white plume (symbol of his honor) unsullied. Dr. Bob Jones—the fighting Fundamentalist, the artist, the jokester, the kind and generous friend—has gone to his heavenly home with his white plume unsoiled.

His was a lifetime of consistency. Even his greatest enemies must admit to and admire his consistent stand for his faith.

Cyrano said, "And tonight when I enter God's house, in saluting, broadly will I sweep the azure threshold with what despite of all I carry forth unblemished and unbent . . . and that is . . . my plume!"

With his testimony unblemished.

With his Fundamentalist position unbent . . . our great and noble warrior enters the azure threshold and stands before his beloved Lord with his plume unsullied.

Bobbie Yearick

What's in a name? So much! Especially if that name is Dr. Bob Jones Jr. My first knowledge of him came from a young naval officer following a Youth for Christ service in Charleston, South Carolina. During a casual conversation he related that he would finish his tour of duty in a few weeks and then continue his graduate work at Bob Jones College. He wanted to go there because he had heard about a very famous actor, writer, and preacher who was connected with the school. His words were, "I want to meet him and learn from him."

It was some months later when I learned from the naval officer that Bob Jones College was going to move to Greenville, South Carolina, and that I might be able to get a job in their offices. Most of his letter, however, talked about Dr. Bob Jones Jr. His glowing report about Dr. Bob's acting abilities, his skillful handling of the Word, his powerful preaching, and his keen mind (never needing to use the hymnbook when singing in services) created in me a real desire to know this unusual person.

When the school came to Greenville, I did get a job in the office. Can you imagine how I felt when I was given the privilege to take dictation from him? (It was not a regular responsibility but an occasional one.) All was well until he used "ecumenical" in a sentence. Never had I been exposed to that word. His secretary graciously helped me when I did the translating. She knew I would encounter it many times.

One day Dr. Bob came into the large typing room, walked over to my desk, and asked me to come into his office for a few minutes. He settled my fears when he asked me if I would like to continue my college education. Even though he knew I had no money, he said that I would be allowed to work my entire way through. What an answer to prayer! When I was fifteen, my widowed mother and I stopped our work in a cotton field and knelt down and asked God to make it possible for me to get a college education. God used this choice servant of His to give me the desires of my heart.

As I had been told and envisioned in my own mind, Dr. Bob was a great actor, inspiring writer, powerful preacher, and educator; but he was so much more. He was tender and kind and had an unusual ability to sense the needs of people and do something about it. I observed such traits as he interacted with his family, his friends, and strangers.

How often he preached great classical sermons. But none could rival his "visits" with us. On one of those days, while we met in the old gym as the auditorium was being completed, he reminded us of the little lad with five loaves and two fishes. It was as though he looked up the bleachers and directly at me when he said, "Young people, you may not have more than loaves and fishes. But God wants that." It was that day that I stopped my struggle and complaining about my lack of talent and surrendered everything in my life to the Lord. The great orator never preached a more meaningful sermon!

A number of years ago my husband and I had taken my aunt to the train station in Greenville. We were delighted to see Dr. Bob Jr. there and learn that he, too, was going to Washington, D.C. I introduced him to Aunt Gladys, and within a few minutes the conversation was turned to the Lord. He knew at once that she perhaps was not saved. That was the way he was—always interested in the salvation of souls.

When we last visited Dr. Bob, he said to Dave, "We owe you two a meal (that was not true, of course), but we will have to have it at the Marriage Supper of the Lamb." He then autographed a book for our daughter, Marla, who is in Africa. He needed his glasses, and when I placed them on his face, I remarked about his drugstore ones. He said, "I'm not going to spend money on expensive glasses." It was another reminder of how "down-to-earth" he was. We all know how he disliked glasses.

He asked about each of our children that day and made some comment about them. It was a reminder again that he had a genuine love for people. Never a pretense. How we miss him!

Elizabeth Edwards

I have known Dr. Jones for sixty-three years—first as my teacher of history and speech, where I learned so much and have many memories of the classes with him.

When I joined the faculty in 1939, it was very natural we would become good friends since Dr. Jones and my husband already were. Each was the other's best man at our weddings. Within a year, when the Joneses first child arrived, we became baby-sitters, as they would let us. Then came the pleasant memories of seeing our children grow up together.

Through the years there were many pleasant memories of our acting together in films and in Shakespeare. There I gained knowledge of directing and acting. Dr. Jones was a prankster, and in a production of *Merchant of Venice,* when I was Portia and he was Shylock, in the court scene Portia was disguised as a lawyer, Shylock held out the bond to prove his right to a pound of flesh from Antonio, and there he had written in bold letters, "You can't fool me. I know who you are."

As I taught speech over fifty years, I used his sermons as excellent examples of a good speaker—his knowledge of the Scripture, wisdom in conveying it, word choice (part of which was acquired from familiarity with the best of literature—the area I was teaching), his imagination to make these images come alive, and his love for souls.

Dr. Bruce McAllister

One day on a plane with Dr. Bob and Mr. Tony Miller, we were enjoying relaxed conversation. For a while we talked about Alabama, and Dr. Bob knew so much about life in north Alabama, which is my home area. Then Dr. Bob and Mr. Miller talked extensively about Australia, which both men knew well. Next Dr. Bob told us a story about the garden tomb in Jerusalem. Dr. Bob had been bothered by some neglect he had noticed at the garden tomb and decided to write the responsible party in Great Britain. He accomplished positive change as a result of his letter. I came away from that plane amazed at how Dr. Bob knew so much about places and people in different corners of the world and even knew how to get improvements made at the garden tomb in Jerusalem! I am sure that the half has not been told.

Dr. Bob Wood

Proverbs 16:31 says, "The hoary head is a crown of glory, if it be found in the way of righteousness." I often think of that verse when I think of Dr. Bob Jr. Over the last twenty years I have had the opportunity to have many informal conversations with him here in the office. I heard much about the history of Fundamentalism and the evangelism of days gone by. I consider it a great privilege to have had a personal course in "The History of Fundamentalism" from the "Dean" himself. Also, it was obvious to me that the Lord had given Dr. Bob a very special gift of discernment. Through the years, he made many predictions about men in ministries that have all turned out to be true. What a wonderful gift the Lord gave him to see the future. I will always cherish the memories of these personal conversations, and I will never get over the impact they have made in my life.

Willie Thompson

I shall never forget the kindness of Dr. Bob and Mrs. Jones during his illness. I stopped by unannounced to encourage him but went away a greater debtor to him than what I was before I arrived.

Mr. Stephen Jones arrived at the same time I did and checked to see if his grandfather were up to having a visitor so early in the morning. When he returned, he said Dr. Jones would see me. It was my intention to go by to assure him that the WMUU Powerhouse [radio program] audience was praying for him and to thank him for all that he has meant to me and my family over the years. He greeted me with a handshake and offered me breakfast, which, at the first and second offers, I turned down because I had planned on staying only a minute or two. At the third or fourth offer to have breakfast with him, I accepted the breakfast prepared by Mrs. Jones. During breakfast we talked about various aspects of serving the Lord and our testimonies of salvation. When we talked of his illness, he said, "I asked the Lord not to let me stay around here if He has nothing else for me to do." The Lord certainly answered his prayer. We ended the visit with prayer together.

I walked out of his house thinking, he's the one in pain; yet his pain has not dimmed his vision for serving the Lord, resting on His promises, and being kind. However, I was not surprised that he talked of the Lord and salvation He provides. For that is what his life has been to me since I enrolled in BJU in September 1975. I praise the Lord for Dr. Bob Jones Jr.'s ministry.

Sue Tabler

It has been my great privilege to have known Dr. Bob Jones Sr., Dr. Bob Jones Jr., and Dr. Bob Jones III personally. I count this as one of the biggest blessings of my life.

When I came to Bob Jones University as a very green seventeen year old and began working in the Administration Building three days after graduating from high school, everything was new and impressive to me—the campus, the work, and especially the people.

My little community didn't provide opportunities to "rub shoulders" with people of talent and greatness very much, so I stood in awe of many people at BJU—and still do.

The first memory of a personal contact with Dr. Bob Jr. was shortly after I arrived. I was sent to look up something in the files and was writing the information on the piece of correspondence laid out on the file cabinet so, therefore, had my arms resting on top of the cabinet. This proved too much of a temptation for Dr. Bob Jr. as he happened by, and he gave me a good poke in the ribs from each side. Since I am extremely ticklish, this jolt was not to my liking at all; and I whirled around to confront the culprit. However, my indignation vanished when I saw my tormentor was Dr. Bob Jr., who was smiling at me with a very pleased and impish glint in his eye. He thought I was going to faint because I always turn pale rather than red when I am embarrassed.

Having worked all these years in the Administration Building, I have seen Dr. Bob Jr. in many settings and under many circumstances. More than once I have seen him go to extraordinary lengths and even "bend over backwards" to make sure he was being completely fair to people who, in anybody's book, had some personality traits which were less than admirable. He wanted to make sure neither he nor the others involved judged these people by their unattractive characteristics but, rather, reached their decision based on the facts and governed by what was right and not emotion.

Dr. Bob had great compassion, which was expressed freely in his letters, in his preaching, and in personal contacts. Some years ago, Corban's father had a serious heart attack on a Sunday morning. We quickly made plane reservations for him to go to his father's bedside; and as we were waiting at the airport for Corban's flight to be called, Dr. Bob Jr. came into the waiting area on his way to his own flight. My first impulse was, "There is Dr. Bob. Ask him to pray for Papa." I had no hesitation about calling out his name, running to where he was, and pouring out our prayer request to him. My children thought I was rather bold and forward to waylay **The Chancellor** in this manner, but I had no qualms about the reception

Dr. Bob would give me or my need. Dr. Bob expressed genuine concern, and his promise to pray for us helped to calm my heart and mind during the time of distress, and I am sure he did pray for Papa during his flight. Papa recovered.

There were many examples showing Dr. Bob's remarkable mental abilities. Just one example was when I was assigned a certain job which made it necessary for me to check procedures with him fairly frequently. I would carefully type out the problem and ask for his solution. On several occasions I was directed to take the paper to him at his desk. He would take it in his hand and almost in the same motion hand it back and give me specific instructions about what to do. I felt there was no way he could have even read it in that short amount of time, much less formulate an answer. However, every time as I followed through on his instructions, I could tell he had read the problem, digested its contents, and had given me the proper solution.

Dr. Bob liked to tease and banter with people, but he didn't like for it to be all on his side—he liked for the person to "give it back to him." There was one secretary in the Executive Wing, whose last name happened to be Jones, with whom he especially enjoyed kidding. Once he was talking about his "Shakespearean diaphragm," and she was teasing that he was getting paunchy; so he drew in his "Shakespearean diaphragm" and told her to hit it. And she did—but not very hard. He encouraged her to make it harder, and she did that. He walked away with a very pleased expression on his face because she was surprised at how solid it was. The rest of us were surprised that she would even in jest dare to punch him! When this same girl became engaged over the Christmas holidays and was showing off her ring, Dr. Bob said with a real twinkle in his eye, "Did he kiss ya?" To which she replied with emphasis, "Yes, *several* times." I don't think he was expecting such a fervent answer and muttered, "Well, I hope your mother was there," and left. His comment to her after another give-and-take conversation was, "You act like a Jones."

Not being very good at bantering, I can recall only one time when I "won." He came strolling into our office, as we so much enjoyed to have him do, and I said, "Dr. Bob, a member of your family is walking down the sidewalk." He hurried over to the window and looked out expectantly. He said he didn't see any member of his family, and I pointed to a long-haired white cat named Charlemagne, which I think belonged to Beneth. He turned away in disappointment and a little disgust, too, since he was not known for his love of cats.

My last conversation with Dr. Bob Jr. and the last time I saw him was after he had had the pacemaker installed but before his diagnosis of cancer. His sense of humor was still in top shape, although his body was beginning to show signs of weakness. He said he was just so tired that his feet didn't want to pick up. He told me he had just been to the doctor, and the doctor had asked if he exercised. He said, "I told him, 'Yes, I run.' " Then came the dramatic pause during which I registered the surprise he was expecting from me. He continued: "I told him, 'Anytime anyone suggests exercise to me, *I run!*' "

Iris Jackson

The first time I ever saw Dr. Bob was when he walked out under a spotlight on a dark stage in a white suit to read "Aux Italiens" on Vespers in the spring of 1942. The elegance of his appearance was overshadowed only by the eloquence of his speech. As the lights came up at the end of the program, I felt I had "died and gone to heaven." Never in my wildest imagination could I have dreamed I would have the privilege of knowing this great man and working with him for over fifty-five years.

My first introduction to him as a very practical man came in the summer of 1947 when he and Mrs. Jones, with their three young children, were loading up the car to head for their new home in Greenville, South Carolina. After a rather agonizing time of getting all the children, their toys, and the necessary accoutrements for a young family's all-day trip through the mountains tightly packed in and the car doors closed, Dr. Bob opened his door and firmly announced, "Now, everyone get out and go to the bathroom because it's going to be a long ride, and I'm not going to be stopping every few minutes!"

Over the years, I was privileged to hear Dr. Bob preach all of his sermons, some, of course, many times. My favorite would have to be "What Shall We Have Therefore?" since it spoke to my heart so forcefully of the need for total surrender to God's will in every matter. I was always amazed at the effectiveness of his quiet manner of giving invitations—no singing, no protracted pleading—just the organ playing quietly as the Holy Spirit worked and people responded. How blessed my life has been because of his willingness for God to use him.

His Personal Touch

Vicki Fremont

On my way to school from Nebraska in 1980, my first year at BJU, my mother and sister were in a terrible car crash before I had even left the state of Nebraska. My mother nearly died in that crash. She knew that it was important that I stay in school and *insisted* that I stay! Dr. Bob made an effort to meet me, and each time he saw me around the campus, he always stopped me and asked me how my mother was coming along and assured me that he was praying for her, for me, and for my family. That touched not only my heart but the hearts of my parents as well. They remember his sincere concern during that time!

Rev. Dale Leathead

For three years I had an opportunity during my student days to work quite closely with Dr. Bob as part of the stage crew for the Classic Players. My last year at BJU I was assistant stage manager for the annual productions and, of course, had an even closer contact with him than in the previous years. After graduation I went to Asia as a foreign missionary, where I served for eighteen years. I was physically out of touch with happenings and personnel at BJU during those years. In 1973 (twenty-five years after graduation) I attended a summer banquet in the area where I was living at the time, and Dr. Bob was the speaker. I approached him after the event and was so impressed with the fact that he knew me by name after all those years! What a memory he had!

Babbett Hagans

As a student, I worked in the Blue Room as a hostess. I am thankful to have had the opportunity to serve Dr. Bob and to witness many of the qualities that made him so dear to so many people.

Dr. Bob disliked cheesecake. When we served it at a meal, he would take one bite to be polite; and after the meal was over, he would poke his head into the kitchen and tell us girls that he had touched it once with his clean fork and we should be sure to eat it so it wouldn't go to waste.

I also remember setting up for meals where the guests had to cancel at the last minute due to conflicts. Instead of wasting the food, he would ask us to go to the varsity lobby to invite students to come and eat. What fun it was to see the surprised expressions of the people we asked to come to the Blue Room for supper!

One of the dearest memories I have is of Dr. Bob sharing the need of a Savior to a guest before the meal began. He spoke to this man of his need for the Savior and told him how to be sure of going to heaven when he died. Dr. Bob introduced the guest to the Savior with the love and gentleness of one who knew our Savior intimately. Being present at that moment, I witnessed an example of the relationship that Christ wants us to have with Him.

Melody Jones

Dr. Bob meant so much to me; he truly was the "grandpa of BJU." I will always remember his speaking in chapel, especially when he went off on tangents talking about dogs and about things he got in trouble for when he was a student here at BJ.

He had such a sweet and kind heart. I remember one time when I was flying back to BJU from Detroit. I was standing in line to make sure my ticket was all set, and right in front of me Dr. Bob was standing waiting. He had been in another state preaching, and due to the weather, they had to drop him off in Detroit. I asked him if he wanted to sit with my family and me, and sure enough, he came over and chatted with my family as we waited for our plane.

When we got to the Greenville airport, Dr. Bob saw that I had lots of things to carry, and he grabbed my very heavy book bag that was filled with books. He was such a gentleman! Dr. Bob had a problem, though. He wasn't able to get hold of his wife to come pick him up due to his flight change. Well, Dr. Bob ended up riding back with me in a friend's car. He told us lots of stories about his experiences in visiting other countries and all of the different foods that he had tried. He had a wonderful sense of humor. He kept us laughing almost the whole way back.

Mrs. Howard Schlichting

My friend, Mrs. Barbara Van Pelt, was visiting here from New England this past January. She had heard a lot about the University and was anxious to see it. She had always been interested in the theater, but throughout her life, many people in the church tried to convince her that it was ungodly. When we visited Rodeheaver [Auditorium], she about went to pieces with delight. We must have spent two hours there. Everyone was so helpful in explaining or showing her anything she asked about. The costume room was the last place, and she just could not tear herself away. In fact, the staff stayed on their own time to finish talking with her. She was to leave the next afternoon.

That morning at breakfast we were chatting, and I said, "Is there anything you wished you could have done while you were here?"

She said, "Oh, yes, but it is an impossibility!"

I said, "Well, tell me; maybe it isn't."

"I would just love to talk with Dr. Bob Jr. about the theater work at BJU," she said.

So I replied, "Well, I will call him and see if he might have a few minutes to talk."

She said, "Do you know him?"

I said, "Not personally, but I know of him; and if he can, he will." So I called, and he said to come by after lunch. Well, I will never forget the brilliance on her face.

[Dr. Bob] graciously met us at the door, and we sat in his office chatting for well over an hour. The time just flew by. I was home schooling my eighth grader, Jason, at the time, so, of course, he joined us. Unbeknownst to your dad, Jason just loved going to chapel to listen to him and was just as excited about this adventure as Barbara. He told your dad about the time we saw him on campus with this flamboyant tie, shirt, and jacket combo. Dr. Bob went on to tell how people send them as gifts to him, and he does not want to make anyone feel bad, so he wears them. We had a nice chuckle, and, of course, Jason just hung on his every word the whole time.

Dr. Dan Turner

As a married senior student in December 1971 I had the opportunity, with the summer ensemble with whom I had traveled, to fly to Boston with the Chancellor to appear on a television program. The shoes I wore had seen better days, and though polished and shined, they had a huge hole in the sole of each shoe. During the taping, the weather in Boston turned ugly with heavy rain and sleet. As we walked from the air terminal to the plane, I dodged puddles and, trailing everyone so as not to be noticed, tried to walk on my toes or heels so that the water would not get in my shoes. Dr. Jones noticed and asked if I had injured myself. When I showed him my shoes, he smiled sympathetically and told me that he hoped I wouldn't get sick. The next day back on campus, I found an envelope in my post office box containing a note which said, "Someone told us you needed a new pair of shoes." Folded in the note was $25. That week I found a very good pair of Florsheim dress shoes on a half-price sale for $22.50. I know that Dr. Bob sent the money for the shoes, and it was a great lesson for me!

Frank Plessinger

Just after we moved to BJU, our family went to eat supper at a local steak house. As we started to eat, Dr. Bob Jr. and Dr. Bob III walked by our table. My youngest daughter of five years waved to them and yelled, "Hi, Dr. Bob!" I told our children not to make a show. "Besides," I said, "we have been on campus only a few months, and I have spoken to Dr. Bob Jr. only once on my way to chapel." At once, Dr. Bob stopped and walked over to our table. He greeted me by my first name and asked the name of my wife and children. He then pulled out of his pocket some candy and gave it to our kids. He went on to say, "Because we look so much alike," as he pointed over to the table where Dr. Bob III had just sat down, "just remember, kids, that I'm the one who hands out the candy!"

Jim Berg

My first up-close encounter with Dr. Bob was my freshman year when I was working at the Information Desk. I was working one of my first Saturdays alone, which is quite a scary thing for a freshman. Dr. Bob walked out of the executive wing of the Administration Building and crossed the lobby to head out the back door for the Art Gallery. As he walked by, he greeted me with, "Good morning, Jim. How are you doing?" I had no idea how he knew my name, and it impressed me that he would go to whatever lengths it took to make someone feel at ease. No one was unimportant to him.

Dr. James Roach

This story took place about ten years ago. Our five-year-old daughter Joy had somehow gotten a sharp sliver-sized piece of metal lodged in the middle of her eye. Her whole eye had turned a strange yellow-red color, and she was crying. My wife was walking her to our car to go to the clinic when Dr. Bob came walking by and stopped to see what was wrong. After expressing his sympathies, he then said that "he would pray" that the Lord would heal Joy. Well, the Lord did heal her miraculously that day, and we never forgot that this kind man would take the time to pray for our little girl in the time of need.

Joe Allen

My first memory of Dr. Bob occurred during the summer after my freshman year (1964). I invited my pastor (non-BJU grad) to a BJ banquet in Indianapolis. Before I could introduce my pastor to Dr. Bob, the Chancellor put forth his hand and said, "Hello, Bob."

After the banquet I asked my pastor how he knew Dr. Jones. He replied that he met him at a preachers' meeting a couple years earlier. Wow! I was amazed how Dr. Bob could remember the name of a pastor of a small church.

Melanie Suydam

One thing that sticks out to me about Dr. Bob is that he paid close attention to details. I remember being introduced to him last year by one of his granddaughters. A short time afterwards I met him again at his house. I usually wear contacts, but for some reason, this time I was wearing my glasses. When I was introduced to him again, he said that he remembered who I was but that the last time he saw me I wasn't wearing my glasses. For a man who was occupied with so many people so much of the time, his observance of this detail really impressed me.

Diane Carter

In his own testimony, which was printed in the program at the celebration of his home going, Dr. Bob stated, "One of the great joys I have had in life, possibly my greatest joy aside from my family. . . ." When I think of Dr. Bob, my first thoughts are not of him as the Chancellor of Bob Jones University, or the evangelist, the Shakespearean actor, the art connoisseur, or a poet. My first thought is of the man who, next to his Lord, loved his family foremost. You could sense that love whenever he spoke of his family.

I've never forgotten the first time that I became acutely aware of how much Dr. Bob loved his family, collectively and individually. It was during an evening meal about ten years ago. Everyone was interacting in the table conversation, and I observed Dr. Bob as he singled out each family member. He asked them about their day, but he also challenged them with questions and ideas. I remember his discussing art with one of his grandsons and commenting that the two of them should make a trip together to view a particular artwork. This was not idle talk with Dr. Bob. Actually, very little talk with Dr. Bob was idle. He had a wealth of knowledge about many subjects, and it was natural for him to share that knowledge and challenge you to think. He teased his daughter-in-law, which he did often; but the love and the pride he had for her was very evident. I've never gotten away from what I observed that night. My love and respect for Dr. Bob, the family man, was enhanced.

Another event that I remember particularly occurred one evening as the Jones family was leaving the Blue Room in the Dining Common. I was on staff in the Dining Common at that time. The family preceded Dr. Bob down the stairs. He lingered behind them and began to talk. He commented about Mrs. Jones Sr.'s failing health and then he said, "You know, I believe that Mom will live to be a hundred." She was in her early nineties at that time. He made this statement with complete sincerity and conviction. I never doubted but that she would live to be a hundred years old. Mrs. Jones died when she was one hundred years and seven months old.

What could be said about Dr. Bob's love and tenderness toward his wife could be told justifiably only by her. But his love for Mrs. Jones was evident in his words and actions, even to the most casual observer.

Dorreene Holmes

I have so many fond memories of Dr. Bob that it is next to impossible to tell in any sort of brief way his impact on my life. Dr. Bob and Mrs. Jones were married at the end of my freshman year in college in Cleveland, Tennessee, and all these sixty and a half years at BJC and BJU have been filled with blessings.

When my mother died in 1975, just before Christmas, the hospital notified Dr. Bob (as Barge often does when there is a death there). He told them not to call me and tell me but that he wanted to come and tell me personally. I had left the hospital about a half-hour earlier that night. Mother seemed to be resting and feeling fairly well. We had read a psalm and had prayer, and she told me to go home, that she would be all right. Dr. Bob got a friend to come with him to CVA and prayed with me. It was so comforting. I knew Mother was in heaven, but Dr. Bob's coming at that time, when he was busy with Christmas activities, etc., with his family, meant so much. It was really touching. He was so interested in all people. He was so humbly great!

Dr. Dwight Gustafson

I worked closely with Dr. Bob in administrative details and in a multitude of Fine Arts activities from the time I first designed stage sets for him in my sophomore year in college (1950) right on through all these years until now.

His quest for excellence was unalterable. Every detail of a stage production had to be absolutely accurate. I once got a single-spaced, full-page memo concerning accuracy after a pair of canvas tennis shoes (properly decorated, of course) was seen on an actor in a production of Gounod's *Faust*. That same determination to be absolutely correct was present in all he did. He despised sham and put-on, not only "on-stage" but also in every aspect of life and Christian living. That trait has borne fruit in all aspects of the University's life.

He was "in charge," but at the same time he could be completely selfless in his generosity. One day backstage after chapel in Rodeheaver Auditorium I admired a new, black leather coat he had just brought back from a trip to the Middle East. He immediately said he wanted me to have it. I was embarrassed and protested. He said, "Gus, I have too much of a 'pot' to look good in it." I still protested, but he made me try it on. Unbelievably, it fit perfectly. He said, "I can't give it to you now, but I'll go home and get another coat, and you can pick this up at my office this afternoon." That is just the way he was. He was my boss for nearly forty years, yet he was also my friend. His adherence to principle was as determined as his adherence to the complete truth of God's Word. But at the same time he had a tender heart for the souls of men and for so many that he touched personally.

Steve Skaggs

My freshman year (1981) I was privileged to obtain a small role in *King Lear* with Dr. Bob playing the title role. I was the Duke of Burgundy, appearing in only one scene and having only three lines. I remember the fun I had going back to the dorm after one rehearsal and telling my roommates that Dr. Bob had showed up in jeans! They almost didn't believe me. I also remember the way the audience laughed during a performance when, after Lear's Fool sang a short song, Dr. Bob ad-libbed, "When are you going to learn to sing, Fool?"

I had a lot to learn about acting. I remember one time using a gesture that I thought was appropriate. Extending my hands at waist level and moving them up and down with my elbows slightly bent, I said my line: "Royal King, give but that portion which yourself propos'd." Dr. Bob stopped me. "This gesture," he said, demonstrating from his seat on Lear's throne, "is always a weak gesture. If you see anyone using that gesture, you know he's a poor actor. I call it 'shaking a wet baby.'" His attitude as he said this was one of a grandfather giving blunt but necessary advice. I had to laugh, as did the rest of the cast, but you can be sure I never used that gesture again!

Another incident involving *Lear* was less pleasant. We had blocked the scene a certain way at one rehearsal, and when we came back a few nights later, Dr. Bob recalled the blocking differently from the way I did. I (respectfully, I believed) disagreed, saying something like "I think we came up the ramp before we said our lines." The director pulled me aside a few minutes later and firmly said words I will never forget: "I don't ever want to hear you speak to Dr. Bob like that again!"

I was absolutely humiliated. I had intended no disrespect at all; I had just been trying to help. I took the first opportunity I could to try to make things right with Dr. Bob. Catching him as he left the stage toward the end of the rehearsal, I apologized for what I had said. I could tell from his response that he was genuinely puzzled, not sure to what I was referring. "Well, when I corrected you earlier in rehearsal. I'm sorry for that. I didn't want you to think I was being disrespectful." He just kind of shook his head. He had completely forgotten the incident until I mentioned it. "That's all right. Don't think a thing of it," he said. "We're all just working things out here, making mistakes and learning together." I felt an immediate, immense sense of relief!

When I think of that event now, however, I realize I learned an unexpected, important lesson. I learned that a truly great man is a patient and humble man, not easily offended. In retrospect, this is a more important truth than I would have learned if Dr. Bob had sternly rebuked me, as I no doubt deserved.

Dan Huffstutler

When I was a freshman coming to BJ, I had to leave from Chicago's O'Hare International Airport. When I arrived at O'Hare, my parents dropped me off and had to leave. Unfortunately, I had to wait two extra hours for my plane because it had been delayed. While I was waiting, this elderly man and his wife came and sat next to me. As soon as he sat down, I began thinking, "I have seen this guy somewhere before." But I couldn't remember who he was. I was thinking of all kinds of TV personalities like the old man in the old Smith-Barney commercials who said, "We make money the old fashioned way . . . we *earn* it."

Anyway, after racking my brain for a while and trying to figure out who this guy was, I thought, "Could this be Dr. Jones?" I don't think I had heard him preach when I came as a high school student, so I really don't know how I came to the conclusion that this might be Dr. Bob. I didn't want to ask a total stranger if he were Dr. Bob, so I pulled out all my catalogs and introductory material and began leafing through them and being real obvious with it, hoping he would say something. I was also looking for a picture of him, but I couldn't find one. Finally I found a picture of Dr. Bob III and then tried to look at the picture and compare the elderly man next to me to the picture without attracting too much attention—which was kind of difficult.

This still did not let me know who he was, but I just had this idea that I was sitting next to Dr. Bob. So I sat there trying to think of some cool way to ask a complete stranger, fifty years older than I, if he were Dr. Jones from Bob Jones University.

Finally, I noticed he was coughing and asked him about his health. After a little small talk, I asked him if he was Dr. Jones; and, of course, he was. He then proceeded to keep track of me for the next few hours as we flew from Chicago to Atlanta, got delayed again for two hours, and then flew from Atlanta to Greenville. While waiting in Atlanta, he bought me lunch and answered all my millions of questions. Then when we flew from Atlanta to Greenville, I got to sit next to him and ask him another million questions. I had a great time. I couldn't believe that I, as a freshman, had run into Bob Jones in the middle of O'Hare Airport and was riding all the way back to BJ with him.

When we arrived in Greenville, he made sure I made it to the bus and got squared away. Bob IV was there to pick him up, but Dr. Bob kept checking up on me to make sure I got on the bus, etc. It was quite an experience to meet the Chancellor of BJU on the way to BJU for college. It really confirmed in my mind God's plans for my life. I was struck with his kindness and generosity as he bought me lunch, made sure I got through all the different terminals, answered all my questions about planes and clouds and other stuff, and generally treated me like his grandkid. It's a great memory.

Wendel Alewine

I work as a staff member in the Administration Building. Several years ago during one very busy week, I found a quiet, lonely couch down in the lower wing after office hours and was taking a quiet rest. Dr. Bob came in the building and "caught" me. I was not quite sure what to expect, but he seemed to understand my fatigue and told me to "take off your shoes and put your feet up and rest." I was thankful for his kindness.

Pat LeMaster

From the day we came to work at BJU in 1989, I was impressed with Dr. Bob's love for children. Our daughter, Joanna, was in the third grade that year, and she loved Dr. Bob right from the start. During the summer when all the faculty and staff ate in the Varsity Room together, she would make it a point to talk to Dr. Bob at almost every meal. I had to limit her visiting times to one to two minutes because she enjoyed talking to him so much. He never acted put out or upset that his meal was interrupted. He always was very congenial and made her feel quite important. I don't suppose he ever knew how much he meant to her. Even though she is now sixteen, she still considers herself his "little buddy," a name he gave her years ago.

Vicky Robbins

One of my fondest memories of Dr. Bob was backstage at the opera my freshman year. During the second performance, he came through the Green Room on his way back to listen to one of his favorite parts of the opera. Of course, he took the time to stop for a few minutes and chat with us. At one point he noticed that there was a guy wearing a boutonniere and asked him why he had it on. He told Dr. Bob that he was playing in the off-stage trumpet ensemble; and since he was not able to attend the performance with his girlfriend that evening, she got him the boutonniere. Dr. Bob made a comment about how sweet that was, and then a girl asked, "Where's *your* flower, Dr. Bob?" And he said, "Oh, she's at home."

Hannah Bixby

When I heard the news that Dr. Bob had passed on to be with the Lord, one of the thoughts that went through my mind was that one of his dreams had finally come true.

I remember so many times in chapel after an especially enthusiastic song service Dr. Bob would get up and say, "You know, I wish I could sing. God didn't see fit to give me a good singing voice, but when I get to heaven, God is going to give me a perfect voice so that I can sing praises to God right along with the angels." Dr. Bob is probably singing at the top of his lungs right now!

His Humor

Dr. David Yearick

In the first full-length film produced by Unusual Films back in 1950, *Macbeth,* Dr. Bob played the title role, and I played Macduff. The climax of the story is when Macduff kills MacBeth in a sword fight. In the film, we were to do this on horseback. Since neither one of us was a great swordsman or great equestrian, the whole picture could have turned out to be a comedy instead of a tragedy. We ran at one another and made a less-than-majestic clashing of

---

swords. After several takes, Mrs. Stenholm, the director, decided that most of the duel would be better done on foot than on horseback. Even that was kind of pathetic, but with the help of a good editor, there was enough acceptable footage to complete the film.

On several occasions I assisted Dr. Bob with weddings and funerals. Only once can I recall that we had both on the same day, and I kept teasing him about being careful not to use the wedding notes at the funeral and the funeral notes at the wedding. He never liked to introduce a couple at the close of the wedding, insisting that it wasn't necessary because everybody already knew who they were or they wouldn't have come to the wedding. Therefore, when we did weddings together, he always had me make the introduction.

Mrs. Phil Aguilar

(Written to Dr. Jones during his illness)

Do you, [Dr. Bob], remember your fiftieth birthday that Phil and I celebrated with you in Austin, Texas? You were holding meetings in a Norwegian church, and Phil and I visited the meetings every night. We decided to give you a birthday party, since turning fifty is "right-down-special." You also came to eat Sunday night supper at our little home. I asked you what you would like to have to eat that evening, and you said you would love to have bacon and eggs! You said you couldn't eat them very well of a morning, but you were craving them. I remember that you came out to our tiny kitchen to talk to me, and I accidentally burned the bacon! We ate it anyway! You were so tall, and you stood with your arm leaning on the top of the refrigerator, and I kept thinking, "Oh, that is the *only* place in the house that I didn't dust!"

You were always calling me "Stormy" because of my maiden name, "Tempest." One time I was going up the stairs and you were coming up a few steps behind me. You teased me about being "hefty," and it made me a little peeved with you, and I told you so by patting your extended stomach and saying, "My daddy has an answer for you." You said, "What does your daddy say?" Then I said, "He says some people are pushing it, and some people are pulling it!" You laughed so big and told me, "Stormy, I wouldn't tease you if I didn't like you a lot!"

Vickie Faucette

I cannot tell you how much I admired/loved (*agape*) your father. I wrote to him in early October, and though I know hundreds of pieces of mail were sent, I hope he was yet able to read our mail and hear with his own ears just how much he was loved. I reminded him of the wonderful time we had aboard ship while cruising the Greek Islands and on to the Holy Land. I also reminded him of the "phony" interview I had conducted with a video camera. He told me his name was "Reynolds" and that he was an "ambassador." I've thought many times since that, though said in jest, your father was indeed an ambassador—one representing a heavenly city, with a special calling from God. What a wonderful legacy to leave, and what a marvelous welcome he must have had as he met his Savior face to face just yesterday!

Dr. Thomas Coleman

As a young college student, I remember [Dr. Bob] as a curious mix of an awe-inspiring yet grandfatherly man who really enjoyed the students. Sometimes grandfathers are mischievous, and Dr. Bob was no exception. I still think of the time I was walking across the campus, head down, deep in thought. I went to cross a street. All of a sudden, there was the loud blast of a car's horn, and I was visibly startled. I looked for the offending party only to see Dr. Bob behind the wheel and with an unmistakable grin of satisfaction. All at once, I found myself pleased instead of irritated.

Jon Daulton

Dr. Bob came to hold a week of revival meetings at my dad's church in Chicago when I was in elementary school. We were providing his evening meals at our home. The first night, my mom had been busily preparing the meal, wanting to be sure to be a good hostess. She set the table, we all sat down, prayed, and began to eat. As the food was being passed around the table, Dr. Bob noticed that one of the vegetables was broccoli. As he took the serving dish, he commented (in his inimitable way), "You know, down South we used to smoke broccoli!" Well, mom swallowed hard, and we all had a good laugh, and we'll never forget that day.

Dr. Ken Hay

The first time I asked Dr. Jones to speak at The WILDS it was at a family camp. Dr. Jones had not seen The WILDS and let it be known that he really was not fond of camps. When we took him to his room, he and Mrs. Jones were amazed that The WILDS was not his typical idea of a camp being a muddy pond and a lean-to. Dr. Bob III kidded me that in order to make his father feel at home, we needed to have neon lights flashing outside the window since most of his stays away from home were in city hotels. We all were shocked when Dr. Jones came out the first full day dressed in blue jeans and a University of Pittsburgh football jersey. If there had been any barriers between our staff and the campers, they were broken. The last evening of camp the operational staff did a program for the campers, and Mrs. Jones confiscated the University of Pittsburgh shirt from their room. Mac Lynch stuffed himself with pillows and did a little routine on the platform as though he were Dr. Jones. It was one of the funniest moments that we have had in our dining room over the years.

Blair Frye

I remember when I was in *Prologue* in the spring of 1996, and one of my duties was to strip the holy garments off of John Huss and condemn his soul to the Devil. Well, after one of the rehearsals, Dr. Bob came up to me in the Green Room and talked with me. He asked me how I was but soon got down to business. He told me I had to hate John Huss and really put emotion and feeling into it. He said to really shout out the line and point to Huss and hate him with all that I had in me. I remember leaving him and smiling and saying to myself, "Whoa, I have to hate Dr. Bob III."

Another time that makes me smile was during Gold Rush Daze when I was privileged to have been waked up by Dr. Bob for breakfast. I slept until nine o'clock, and hearing a knock on the door, I got up to answer it. When I opened the door, there was Dr. Bob with a barber-shop-quartet-type styrofoam hat on. He held out this box of donuts to me and said, "Anybody in there hungry for breakfast?" I remember shutting the door and waking up my roommates and announcing that Dr. Bob was at the door!

Mrs. Tim Jones

(Written to Dr. Jones while he was ill)

I graduated from the SAS in Day-Care Ministry. I had to work my way through school. I got the honor of working in the Red Room [in the Dining Common]. The first time I ever had to wait on you I was so nervous. Most people who are in high authority are rude and demanding, but you were far from that. You were kind and thoughtful. One of my fondest memories of you concerns one day after a business luncheon when a friend and I were out on the balcony, outside the Red Room. We were getting ready to drop ice chips on some guys who were below. What we didn't know was that you were behind us. You asked us what we were up to, and then you came up with a plan. You told me to drop the full cup of ice (except the glass) on the count of three. I did, and when the guys looked up, who did they see but you! You leaned over the ledge and chuckled at them.

That fun-loving side of you is what God used to show me what a wonderful person you are. He knew I had to see that so I would listen when you talked. And in chapel that is exactly what I did. You brought so many changes in my life through your preaching. The most prominent was surrendering my life to God's will and not my will. Another very important lesson I learned was to "keep on keeping on."

Tamar Pundys

Dr. Bob was a prankster. He had a wonderful sense of humor and knew how to make the most of a situation. When I was about twelve, he came to my hometown to speak at a conference at my church. My parents invited my pastor and Dr. Bob over for dinner after one of the services. I'd helped my mom prepare the "spread" and had set the dining room table for the occasion. I was going to be seated to Dr. Bob's left. When we all gathered to the table, he pulled the chair out to seat me. Needless to say, my brothers never seated me, so this was a new experience for me. I must have sat down too soon, so when he went to push the chair in, it got a little "stuck" on the carpet. He decided to capitalize on the moment and let out a big groan as he attempted to push my chair in. My face turned bright red, and he just laughed and laughed! Dr. Bob's zest for life and great sense of humor are some of the things I loved most about him.

Wanda Paddock

Dr. Bob always had mirth surrounding him. Once while we were in Mexico, he suggested that Argyle and I be his guests at a dinner which included all the missionaries in that area. It was a lovely restaurant, and when the waiter came to take orders, Dr. Bob pointed to me and said, "I'm paying for my mother's meal and that man over there!" The waiter came promptly to me and said, "Mother, what would you like?"

Jessica Andersen

I was performing once on a Sunday afternoon Vespers and was wearing a trendy formal gown which featured a knee-length front and a floor-length back. Dr. Bob relieved my jitters by making me laugh as he walked by me backstage, commenting, "Yo' hem's uneven, honey."

Dr. Ken Hay

Our family had the privilege of being in Israel with Dr. and Mrs. Jones several years ago. At breakfast one morning, Dr. Jones was bragging about the yogurt he had just eaten. He declared that it was the best he ever remembered eating and was recommending it to my wife. When he pointed out the yogurt on the buffet bar, my wife discovered that it was sour cream. He was much taken back about that and could not believe it. His wife said that he hated sour cream. Needless to say, my wife did not indulge in the "yogurt" that morning.

Rev. Mike Elder

My days were always brightened by [Dr. Bob's] humor and wisdom. I thank God for his influence on my life. I worked on night watch one summer; and when I was behind your home after midnight, [Dr. Bob] jumped out the back door and nearly scared ten years off my life.

John Weathers

As the weekend mailman, I had the pleasure to be in the mailroom when Dr. Bob would come to work. He would carefully unlock the glass doors and quietly appear in the hallway door and shout, "Boooo!" It would surprise me to no end. We would always have a good laugh, and he would do it again the next time I had weekend duty. I'll miss those precious mornings in the future, but the memory of Dr. Bob will only grow sweeter until the day I surprise him in heaven's mailroom.

Dr. Mike White

My fondest memory of Dr. Bob took place about eleven years ago as I was walking hurriedly from the Administration Building on my way to chapel one sunny morning. The sun in my eyes prevented me from seeing Dr. Bob "moseying" along the covered sidewalk by the Art Gallery, so I clipped along blissfully unaware of his presence. As I drew alongside him, his first comment was, "You know what, son? You move pretty fast for a fat boy!" After the laughter died down and I was heading up the large hill toward the Student Center, he touched my arm and explained, "No, no, son, let's go this way. We fat boys don't like to climb that hill!" And so on we went commiserating about the problems of losing weight until we reached the FMA. I still chuckle every time I think of that episode.

Devvy Walker

I remember Dr. Bob for a lot of things, but one thing that everyone will remember him for often is his sense of humor. I was in the Administration Building with my friend the day before classes started this semester. We were talking to her uncle by the doors that are closest to the Dining Common when I looked back and saw Dr. Bob coming in our direction, about to enter the doors. We kept on talking to her uncle, and Dr. Bob was talking to a lady behind us. All of a sudden I felt a little tug on my hair! I turned around and there was Dr. Bob. He was grinning away and said, "Hi there, how are you doing?" We all just started laughing right then when we realized that I was part of one of his old jokes.

Krystal Godwin

I work in the Executive Wing, and one day as I was coming up the circular staircase in the Wing, I heard a loud thump at the top of the staircase. When I looked up, I saw Dr. Bob standing there. When I got to the top, he said, "Scared ya, didn't I?" I said, "Yes, sir, but wouldn't you have felt bad if you had scared me so much that I fell down the steps?" Dr. Bob looked at me and said, "Yes, I would have." He paused and then said, "I would have had to come down the steps to pick you up!"

Thomas Hitchcock

Every time I think of Dr. Bob, I think about the time when I was still working on stage crew and he came backstage for some reason while we were all talking. He sat down with us at the table and said hello. Before he came, we had been talking about Greek class and how hard it was. Then the conversation changed as we began to say to each other how much we wanted to take Greek and how interesting it was (we did this thinking it would impress Dr. Bob). But to our surprise, Dr. Bob picked up the Greek textbook on the table and said, "I hated Greek." And as we all laughed at his remark, he gave us the most hysterical grin I had ever seen. I will always remember Dr. Bob for his great sense of humor.

Laura Haynes

I remember one time I was in the Dining Common lobby on President's Club day talking to one of the student hostesses. I had my Awana uniform on because it was almost time to meet for extension. Dr. Bob came through on his way up to the Blue Room, and as he passed by, I heard him say, " 'Awana' this, 'Awana' that, just like a woman." That's one of my favorite memories of him.

Angela Merzib

I remember the first time I met Dr. Bob. I was here as a visitor with my parents. A little while before coming to visit the campus we had Dr. and Mrs. Bob Jones III visit our church back home. So when we arrived here, we made plans to meet with them. I remember we had lunch with them in the Blue Room of the Dining Common; and after we had finished our meal, my father wanted to take some pictures. We all got into formation according to his wishes. I was standing in front of Dr. Bob and his wife when I felt a tug on my braid. When I turned around, I saw Dr. Bob standing very composed, so I never suspected he was doing it. A short while later I felt another tug, and when I turned around this time I saw him laughing away!

Wendy Horger

Although I heard Dr. Bob speak many times during chapel, I smile most when I think of the times I saw him in the Family Room of the Dining Common. He was always making a humorous comment to someone as he passed through. Each time I saw him there, I was reminded of his ability to laugh at himself and others. He bore the great responsibility of the University on his shoulders with joy, dignity, and a great sense of humor. His "merry heart" did "good like a medicine" all over campus.

Bryan Ferguson

This story I heard secondhand when I was an undergrad. A student had seen Dr. Bob cut a corner on a sidewalk and walk on the grass, so the student went up to him in jest and asked for his name and ID number. Dr. Bob turned to the student and said, very slowly so it could be written down, "Bob . . . Jones. 2."

Joe Sabbadino

[Dr. Bob] loved to tease. When I was University Host, there was a time I was on the phone at the Information Desk and "someone" threw a paper wad that hit me on the face. Naturally, I was indignant to think that anyone would do such a thing in the Administration Building! I looked up to see who it was and to get ready to do something when I saw Dr. Bob Jr. with a nice smile on his face!

Corretta Grass

It was my privilege to act in many plays with Dr. Bob. Anyone who has had that privilege has been challenged to be word perfect.

Although because of speaking engagements Dr. Bob had to miss many rehearsals, he always knew his lines (as well as almost everyone else's lines) when he came to rehearsals. He enjoyed "acting up" during rehearsals and then would give you that special look during the production which kept you "on your toes" and also kept you wondering if he would do anything funny. One of my most memorable times was during a *Merchant of Venice* rehearsal. It was during the courtroom scene and Portia's famous "Quality of Mercy" speech. Dr. Bob turned his back to the audience, faced me [Portia] squarely and began to "pantomime" everything I said. I tried my best to keep going; however, my voice would shake a little with suppressed laughter until I got in trouble with the director. Dr. Bob was a professional, and everyone learned much about acting skills from his example.

Bill Pinkston

I don't really know if Dr. Jones Jr. was given to winking. But one of the things I remember most about him and will miss the most is his winks.

My first encounter with Dr. Bob was on the stage of Rodeheaver Auditorium. He was performing *Cyrano;* I was a freshman with a two-line bit part, one line of which was between two of his major speeches. During rehearsals, I was always ready to give that short, five-word line, but Dr. Bob did not always give me the cue line. He would often rewrite the speech, skipping my cue entirely. The director, Mrs. Stenholm, called me over before one of the rehearsals and asked why I had not been saying my line. I timidly explained that [Dr. Bob] had been cutting my cue. She then spoke to him, "Bob, he says you've not been saying his cue line. Now don't you go doing that; he's only got two lines." I thought I'd die. But during the rehearsal that evening he again just skipped over my line. Mrs. Stenholm got a hold of me after that rehearsal. "Didn't come anywhere close to your cue line, did he?"

"No, ma'am," I responded.

"Now, what I want you to do is whenever he stops for a half breath, you get your line in."

"Okay," I thought, "he's President of the University, and I'm a freshman. But she's the director." Next time, as he came close to where my speech came in and took "half a breath," I chimed in with my line. He stopped dead in his speech, turned and looked at me, winked, and went on. At the next rehearsal not only did I get my cue line (as written in the script), but I got a wink every time thereafter, even during the performances.

My last wink from Dr. Jones was this summer. I was in his office interviewing him for the Founder's Day program. He was filling in some of the details about his father's ministry, as he told me the story of selling the hymnbooks in the tabernacles and how he would eat onions in order to get to keep the change. He then chuckled and gave me a wink.

Barbara Rumminger

When I first came to BJU in 1945, Dr. Bob did a special performance called "Curtain Calls" almost every year. It was never on the schedule; it would be announced usually at Vespers the Sunday before he planned to give it. He portrayed a variety of classic characters, mostly from Shakespeare, in costume as they appear in a play. We all eagerly awaited this special program. One of the most moving presentations was his representation of Dr. Faustus at the end of life, waiting to be claimed by Satan.

When I was a GA, I was stage manager for the opera *Faust* by Gounod. In the first scene, Satan appears in a flash of light on the last chord of a dramatic sequence. One night when Dr. Bob was watching the rehearsal, it didn't come out exactly right, and he said to me in a very sugary tone, "Sweetheart, if you don't get that cue right, I'll tear your hair out strand by strand and stuff it up your nose!" We got it right!

Anna Turner

I first met Dr. Bob in our Quonset hut church in Waipahu, Oahu, Hawaii. I was in elementary school, and he had stopped to preach in our little church on his way to the Orient. He smiled with a twinkle in his eye and said, "Where do you plan to go to school?" I chirped back, "Bob Jones University!" From that moment, I knew

I wanted to come half a world away from home to this school. God even enabled me to come to the Academy for my junior and senior years of high school.

Attending BJU and flying back and forth to Hawaii each summer were expensive. I had to work during the summers. Unfortunately, summer employment in Hawaii for a high schooler meant only one thing—the dreaded pineapple cannery! I used to love pineapple; but after seeing it, smelling it, and hearing the din of millions of cans being processed, love turned to hate. I no longer *liked* pineapple. On passing through the islands, Dr. Bob asked my parents how things were going for me. They told him how much I now hated pineapple but was willing to bear it so I could go back to BJU. He laughed and dubbed me "the pineapple princess." Years later when I was on-stage during Convocation, Dr. Bob, with that same twinkle in his eye, whispered loudly past all the deans and honorary doctorates, "This is our pineapple princess!" I could only smile and whisper back in a truly shocked voice, "Dr. Bob!" He loved to tease.

Dr. Dan Turner

In the winter of 1987 (I think), Dr. Jones fell on ice while on a preaching tour and broke his hip. Several months after the accident and shortly after he was up and about and was walking without any help, our four-year-old son, Jess, met the Chancellor on the steps of the Family Room in the Dining Common. Jess planted himself firmly on the next-to-the-lowest step, turned around and faced the Chancellor, who was descending the stairs. Jess said, "Bet you can't do this!" and proceeded to jump from the step to the floor. Dr. Bob looked at the four year old and said, "I bet I can!" Before I could say anything, Dr. Jones had launched himself off the step, landed with a slap of his shoes on the tile, and with a smile went off walking out the door toward his office.

Suelane Hannah

A few years ago we had a new nurse at Barge. She knew very little about BJU and had come to work here after marrying a BJ grad who was working on his master's degree. Dr. Bob was a patient at Barge. She went into his room and said, "So, what do you do at Bob Jones?" He graciously replied that he was the Chancellor. She said, "Oh! Well, what does a Chancellor do?" He said, "You are new here, aren't you?" He then proceeded to tell her that when he figured out what a Chancellor does, he would let her know. We teased this nurse for many years about not knowing who Dr. Bob was.

Dr. Rachel Larson

Like most faculty members, I have many special memories of Dr. Bob. One that stands out in my mind relates to the physical beauty of our buildings and Dr. Bob's desire that we be exposed to that which is good and lovely. For fourteen years I had an extension group with the Boys' Bible Clubs at the Salvation Army Boys' Club. Most of our children came from deprived homes. We frequently came to campus. Unlike some of my students, the children had no preconceived notions about art. We made many short trips to the Art Gallery to look at pictures that related to the Bible stories we had recently studied. I remember calling the Art Gallery to ask some questions about locations of specific paintings. I was startled when Dr. Bob answered the phone. I made my inquiry and he answered, and then he teased me, "They are in these galleries now, but next week when *you* get here, they *might* be someplace else. We do change things around here on quiet days because we don't want anyone to get bored. Now tell me again which paintings you're interested in so I can be sure to switch those!"

To my surprise, our short visits to the gallery were a popular activity. One evening when we were at a soccer game and the boys were bored, they begged to go to the gallery and were disappointed when I told them it was closed right then. They called the art they liked most, in the War Memorial Chapel, the "Benjie West Collection." One of the boys told me that it was "Art fit for a king," a truer description than he knew at the moment.

When my workers took their buddies individually to places on campus, we often met in the lobby of the library near the staircase. We met there because it was a spot they loved. They referred to the chandelier as the "angel light" and called the stairs "heavenly

147

stairs." We gathered many times near that angel light on the heavenly stairs. For them it was one of the prettiest places they'd been and it gave us the opportunity to discuss the greater beauties of heaven and how to get there. It was a great blessing to think on things that are good and lovely, and I'm thankful for the vision that made such possible.

Gary Moore

I acted with him in *King Lear.* I played Oswald, a sassy servant. We had a scene where I smarted off to King Lear; and in rehearsal he said, "You know, I think I ought to slap you here; let me try." He slapped me and asked if it hurt. As a freshman, what else could I answer but, "No, that was fine." He slapped me every night and also suggested that I be kicked down the stairs after I die. We had a great time together in rehearsals. He was a blast to act with, and I will always remember him on the stage.

His Character

Dr. Ernest Pickering

I remember working with [Dr. Bob] on productions when I was the student stage manager at the University. I recall well the time when after completion of one of his curtain calls he stepped before the footlights and said, "Some have asked why I left the stage for the pulpit. It has been expressed well in this hymn: 'Were the whole realm of nature mine, / That were a present far too small; / Love so amazing, so divine, / Demands my soul, my life, my all.' " He certainly served God in this manner.

Steve Dempsey

In police terms, your dad was the best. A good cop. A defender of what was right. He knew when to go 10-81 (fight) and when not to. He had the knack to know when to run "Signal 1" (blue lights and siren) and when to go in slow, quiet, no lights. When the 10-41 (need back up) cracks the silence on the radio, he was always 10-5 (on the way) and was 10-6 (arrived at destination) without a 10-50 (accident). When he got there, he was ready and fully prepared to use his 10-49 (gun), if necessary, to eliminate the threat. Your dad was your FTO (field training officer), your partner, and your friend. As a team, you have answered every call imaginable and investigated every type of case, although you will never do another tour of duty with him, 10-19 (meet at a specific location), get another 10-21 (telephone call), or enjoy another 10-13 (meal) with him. He has been reassigned; he is 10-26 (busy), 10-79 (special assignment), 10-20 (location: heaven).

Rev. John Larrabee

When I heard you had only a short time to live, I began to realize that you have, in many ways, been "dead" for a long time. You died to sin when you accepted Christ as a boy. You died to self when you gave up the possibilities of an acting career to enter the ministry as a young man. You died to popularity when, at the height of your personal notability, you took a Fundamentalist stand against Evangelical compromise. Your "deadness" has helped to make Bob Jones University a "dead" place—dead to the latest fads; dead to so-called contemporary Christianity; dead to pragmatism, humanism, and false intellectualism.

As a young pastor, I was on campus for a conference. I came out of the dining hall late one evening as you were leaving your office, and you offered me a ride across campus. During that brief time you spoke with force and passion over your concern that the Jesuit philosophy of "the end justifies the means" had permeated Protestantism and was even having an effect on Fundamentalists. These were not the prepared words of a teacher in class or a preacher in the pulpit. They were the heartfelt personal words of one who saw a clear danger confronting people and things he loved.

I am writing these words as one who, for a time, abandoned the term "Fundamentalist" and dabbled in New Evangelicalism and compromise evangelism. I came to see from the inside the hopeless mess those things produce. I learned the truth that what you win people with is what you win them to, and I became frustrated and disappointed with the emptiness of license in the name of liberty and worldliness in the name of love.

Barbara Lewis

I first met Dr. Bob at a BJU alumni banquet in Puerto Rico in 1973. I was serving as a missionary in another country, and my friend, Beulah Hager, who is a BJU grad, was invited to attend the banquet. She invited me to attend also.

What impressed me most about Dr. Bob was his humor, warmth, concern, humility, and compassion for others. He could have sat with any of the missionaries or pastors, but he chose to sit at a table with the single lady missionaries. He was so tender, cordial, and cultured; such a gentleman. One would have thought by his manner that we were the guests of honor, not he.

He told us many stories and kept us in stitches with his humor. Yet he also demonstrated a real interest and concern in each of us personally and wanted to know about our ministry.

He has always impressed me as someone who stays in the background, not wanting to be noticed but one who gives honor to others; someone who gives his whole heart and attention to those in his presence.

I always looked forward to his preaching in chapel and missed him when he was out running around the world, but I was thankful that the Lord was using him to enrich the lives of others with whom he came in contact. Having known him has made my life richer.

Marsha Mullenax

From the time I was eight years old, I knew I would be attending Bob Jones University. To me there were no other options. I just always knew. Both Drs. Bob were frequent speakers at my church back in West Virginia, so I was exposed to the University from a young age. I remember one visit from Dr. Bob Jr. particularly well because of the impression it made on me and how it reinforced my desire to attend BJ.

I was in junior high and very excited that Dr. Bob was coming. My youth pastor had been promoting the occasion because he was a BJ grad and wanted members of his youth group to attend as well. After the morning service, Dr. Bob was standing at the door shaking hands with people, hugging little children, and commenting that most of the congregation was wearing shoes (surprising, since this was West Virginia) when my youth pastor's three-year-old son got his attention. Dr. Bob picked the little boy up, which pleased the youth pastor tremendously. After all, this was his pride and joy that Dr. Bob was holding. The little boy took a long look at Dr. Bob and declared, "You have *big* lips!" Those of us who heard that observation grew silent, and the embarrassment of the cherub's father was almost beyond description. How could his child have insulted the Chancellor of his alma mater like that?

Dr. Bob didn't appear to be offended, nor did he criticize the youth pastor for not teaching his son to know better than to say such things in public. He merely responded, "You know, I thought the same thing this morning when I looked in the mirror." I couldn't believe that he had been so gracious. He didn't have to be. But in that humble, reassuring response, I saw something I admired. I wanted to spend time at a place that could teach me to be as gracious and kind as that. Surely if the Chancellor of the University had those qualities, the other people in the institution would also. Don't those kinds of traits start at the top? Of course, they do.

I think the thing that impressed me the most at that time and throughout my years at BJU was the ability that Dr. Bob Jr. had to say the right thing. That was a special gift God had given him—the gift of speech—gracious and eloquent, truthful and kind.

Brad Payne

One special memory I have of Dr. Bob dates back to Thanksgiving 1977. As a freshman very much interested in acting, I had the pleasure of being a walk-on in *Merchant of Venice* and seeing Dr. Bob portray Shylock. Three characteristics of Dr. Bob particularly impressed me. The first was his talent. I was amazed at his power of concentration and his ability to transform himself seemingly almost instantaneously into his character. I would stand backstage in awe of how he could be conversing with someone one minute and be on-stage as Shylock the next. The second was his passion for excellence. He was always driven with a desire that each performance be the best it could possibly be. He was quick to notice little things (props, costume accessories, small bits of business) that could be changed to enhance the production. He would offer suggestions and critiques to encourage and compel others to rise to the next level. The third was his humility. He was at ease talking to the stagehands and even us lowly walk-ons, and when he spoke with us, there was a naturalness to the conversation. He never came across as affected or condescending. He showed a genuine interest in others.

His Worldwide Ministry

Rev. James McClelland (Londonderry, United Kingdom)

I shall always have the happiest and the most precious memories of Dr. Bob, as we called him. And I shall always be grateful for his kindness, his influence, and his humility.

All these aspects of his character and more were demonstrated the first time he came to our home. I was a very young minister in Kilkeel, and we were in the middle of building a new church. Dr. Paisley brought him down to see the progress and to have lunch with us. We had a young baby, just about walking age. Running parallel with the path in the back garden was a washing line which, on that day, was filled end to end with diapers that had just been washed and hung out to dry. Dr. Paisley brought your father in through the back gate and along the path beside the washing line. As he came up the path, these diapers were blowing across his face making progress a little difficult. When he got to the back door and met my wife for the first time, he comically quipped, "I see you've got the flags out for us today!"

Dr. Bob was a champion of the Lord's cause, a great friend of those who fought the battle for truth and a most able proclaimer of the glorious gospel. Many thousands of people like myself have good cause to give God thanks for him, for his life, and for having been privileged to have known him. I am just one of that great number.

Dr. Stewart Custer

The memory of serving on missionary trips with Dr. Bob Jones Jr. is a special blessing. In March 1975 Dr. Bob and I went to a missionary conference in Tokyo and Nagoya. As always, Dr. Bob's sermons were great, but behind the scenes he was such a blessing to me and to the missionaries and pastors there. He never seemed to run out of energy. How kind he was. After the conference, he took the speakers and pastors out for dinner at a fancy hotel and picked up the tab for us all. Later I was with him for a missionary conference in Cameroon. Again he was such a blessing to all who were there. He never seemed bothered by the terrific heat. He was so kind to everyone. Audiences perceived him as a stern preacher, but privately he was a kind and gracious man. It was a great privilege to share with him in such service.

Levon Yergatian (Cyprus)

I first met Dr. Bob in 1951 in a car traveling between Larnaca and Nicosia. He was to leave the same day for Israel. In the car he encouraged me to come to Bob Jones. I praise God for that day. I praise God for the education I received; I praise God for the support the University has been to our ministry here and in Armenia.

My four children also graduated from BJ, and from our ministry we have over the years seen more than thirty students also make it to BJ. Currently there are four students finishing their courses. All because of one meeting I had with Dr. Bob in the year 1951.

Dr. David Yearick

When Bobbie and I were in Argentina a couple of years ago visiting missionaries Don and Lois Harris, they expressed a desire to have Dr. Bob visit them but hesitated to ask because they had such a small work. We encouraged them to write to Dr. Bob and invite him to come. He accepted the invitation and in a few months went to preach for them. He stayed in their home. One morning Lois Harris had to go to a ladies' meeting. When she returned, she found that Dr. Bob had washed the breakfast dishes and cleaned up the kitchen and then changed the sheets on his bed before he left. These humble acts on his part made a tremendous impression on them and on the people in their church when they were told about it.

Irina Nunez (Dominican Republic)

I am a freshman at BJU, originally from the Dominican Republic, but I now live here in Greenville. The first time I saw Dr. Bob I was ten years old. He had come over to our school in the Dominican Republic as a guest speaker. When I found out he was such an important man, I was surprised because I would not think a man like Dr. Bob would visit such a small school. It made me realize that to him everyone was the same. To him everyone was special.

My sophomore year of high school I came up here to BJA through my senior year. I am so thankful that I have had the privilege to hear him preach a number of times. He was my favorite. I loved the way he talked to me. He was more of a grandpa than just the Chancellor. Every time he approached the podium, he opened his Bible and talked to us. He made us feel as if we were part of his family. He joked around, he was funny, and he had a sense of humor. Sometimes he was laid back. His messages were so powerful that they spoke to my heart all the time. He will always be remembered. His love for the Lord never changed since the first day that I met him eight years ago until the day he went home to be with the Lord.

Eliezer Yanson (Philippines)

I remember my father telling me how he first met Dr. Bob during a Fundamentalist Congress in the Philippines in the early '80s. At that time my father felt God's call to a full-time radio ministry. He shared this with Dr. Bob, and what an encouragement he was to my father. Knowing that this ministry would be a big step of faith for our family, Dr. Bob gave money to help start the radio program, The Fundamentalist Ministries. Now in its fifteenth year, it is aired on four different radio stations. The program continues to spread the good news and is reaching many lives in the central and southern Philippines.

Dr. Brian Wenham (Australia)

It seemed as though [Dr. Bob] adopted me as one of his boys. I'm only a boy, or that's the way I feel amidst the towering issues of the day; but the Lord gave me a father in the ministry. Your dad was so much like a pastor or a shepherd to me. Sometimes I would express a burden in one of my letters, and the instant reply (he never owed a letter to anyone) would contain the best of godly counsel, just fitted to the need of the hour. I have declared a few times from platforms in Australia, as I have introduced Dr. Bob, "This is my pastor." Having come out of apostasy, I never had any other pastor. Why he adopted me as he did, I cannot fathom, but it has been a privilege to be his Timothy.

A Grandson's Tribute

Bob Jones IV

Editorial for *The Collegian* (BJU campus newspaper)

The joke at my grandfather's seventy-fifth birthday celebration was that he no longer had to worry about dying young. He'd always thought he would, for some reason. As he clocked another decade after that milestone birthday, he often mentioned how amazed he was at his long life. Every year was now a bonus, an extra bit of icing on an already-sweet cake.

But that was his view. Mine was different. To me, Grandpa's continued presence was an entitlement. Like electricity or running water, it was one of those things you can't imagine living without. Eighty-six years wasn't such a long time from my perspective. He had great genes, after all; he was supposed to be around to see my children graduate from college, the way his mother had lived to see my graduation.

Just fourteen hours ago I got the phone call saying he was gone, that he wouldn't even see this year's class graduate, much less the class of 2000-whatever. I'm currently en route to Belfast—in Grandpa's place—to dedicate Dr. Paisley's new church building. Sitting in Frankfurt Airport, I just got another reminder of what an important figure he was in twentieth-century Christianity. Scanning

155

page 2 of *USA Today*'s European edition, a name in bold print caught my eyes. "Bob Jones Jr.," the bulleted item began, "chancellor and chairman of the fundamentalist Christian Bob Jones University, died at age 86. . . ."

Other obituary writers, other historians, won't be so restrained. Grandpa will come in for more than his share of criticism as a leader of a movement that dared to elevate righteousness above relationships. The millions of words he uttered during his long ministry will be weighed in the balances, and most of his critics will find him wanting. "Harsh," "mean-spirited," and "uncompromising" are just three of the labels applied to him during his life. Such criticism surely won't stop now that he's no longer around to defend himself.

Grandpa would have been the first to admit that he was wanting, but not in the way his critics will charge. He weighed himself in the balances every day and always found himself wanting in Christlikeness, in faithfulness, and in a hundred other areas. What he never wanted was the praise of men. The only word of approval he was looking for was the one that he finally heard soon after his body stopped its instinctive fight for that one last painful, rasping breath.

Such a single-minded devotion to his Savior made him absolutely unwilling to bend his convictions for the sake of peace or popularity. Some would say that made him rigid. I disagree. Grandpa may not have bent, but he often stooped. I saw him stoop to admit he was wrong. I saw him stoop to take services in hole-in-the-wall churches that no one had ever heard of when he could have filled his schedule with bigger, more glamorous churches. And most of all I saw the physical stoop in his shoulders when he felt compelled to take a stand that he knew would alienate friends or be misunderstood. He always took the stand he needed to take, but that, in turn, took a lot out of him. For saints or robots it might have been easy, but Grandpa was very human, very much a sinner saved by grace.

Those who never met him in person didn't get to see that side, and so they judged him as harsh. But those who knew him recognized the error in that judgment, even when they disagreed with

Grandpa's principles. The day after he died, our family received a long, impassioned letter from a longtime friend who wanted Grandpa to know how much he'd meant to this man. The writer was an unbeliever, an art dealer from overseas for whom Grandpa had carried a great burden. After saying how much Grandpa meant to him, he continued:

> It is the firmness of your moral conviction, your strength of principle in the doings of life and of the college that are so impressive. Others stick to principle, but I know of no one with principles as rock solid as yours, that are then coupled with so absolute a tolerance of the weaknesses or foibles of others. You once told me that if a friend were in trouble, you would always rise to his support if you agree, and if not, you would pray for him. What a beautiful agenda, which I have tried to adopt, though I am not quite certain of the meaning of prayer.

This man, by his own admission a skeptic in matters of religion, saw in my grandfather's unbending-but-ever-stooping faith something that attracted him. I believe he'll come to Christ soon because of what he saw. To that man, as to me personally, that example is Grandpa's greatest legacy.